SPRING INTO ACTION

A HANDBOOK OF LOCAL FUNDRAISING

Edited by

Martin Field and Alison Whyte

Cartoons by

Sarah De Moratti

MOWBRAY

Mowbray
A Cassell imprint
Villiers House, 41/47 Strand, London WC2N 5JE
387 Park Avenue South, New York 10016–8810

First published 1994

British Library Cataloguing-in-Publication Data
A catalogue record for this book is available from the British Library.

Library of Congress Cataloging-in-Publication Data
Applied for.

ISBN 0–264–67296–8

Front cover illustration by Sarah De Moratti

Phototypeset by Intype Ltd, London
Printed and bound in Great Britain by
Mackays of Chatham. plc

Contents

Foreword and Editors' Note

What do a bishop and his dog in Cornwall, 4,000 plastic ducks in Canterbury, a giant Christmas pudding in Hessle, an old people's lunch club in Hounslow, a hostel for homeless people in Hull and a teenage parents project in Bristol all have in common? The answer is the Church Urban Fund. Set up in 1987 by the Church of England as part of its response to urban need in Britain, the Church Urban Fund has captured people's imagination the length and breadth of England.

Imaginative projects run by local people are bringing hope to some of the most desolate parts of our country. They proclaim that God's love is for all, that the Gospel is practical, real and as relevant and needed in Britain today as it has ever been.

But the imagination and ability to achieve results and to create new life where others see only darkness and despair is matched by those who have given so generously to the Fund to make it all possible.

The Church set itself a daunting £18 million target. In under four years it had exceeded that, making the Church Urban Fund one of the most successful fundraising stories of recent years. Although in some areas grand schemes and specialist fundraisers were at work, most of the money was raised by ordinary people who captured and shared the vision. Many of them had never organized an event before in their lives, but they wanted to do their part to help, to stand alongside their neighbours and contribute what they could. They surprised themselves, not only in the money they raised, but also in the ways in which their church or local community grew as a result.

This book enables others to share this experience and draw on their ideas. Not all these ideas will suit every campaign, not all these ideas will be to everyone's taste – but there are so many here that something is bound to suit.

The secret of the people who worked so hard for the Church Urban Fund? A shared vision, a commitment to share it with others, some down to earth common sense, a willingness to take risks and get their hands dirty. Not so different from living the Gospel, in fact.

+ George Cantuar

Archbishop of Canterbury

This book is dedicated to the memory of Geoff Mann who died, tragically, in February 1993, aged 37. Geoff's personal commitment to the Fund and desire to share his faith with young people today resulted in one of the most distinctive fundraising ideas in this book – *Loud Symbols* (see p. 84) – an expression of his vision, enthusiasm and practical faith.

Our special thanks to all those who helped in writing and compiling this book: Gill Moody, for her excellent fundraising advice and suggestions; Ruth McCurry, for keeping us on the straight and narrow; Maureen Afriat and Ian Keeling for hard work on the manuscript.

Above all, our thanks to everyone who wrote to us with their fundraising stories and ideas. We hope that we've done justice to those we've been able to include and that others will forgive us for those we've had to leave out for lack of space or because they were one of a number of people who had the same idea.

Martin Field
Alison Whyte

1

Making Plans

'What? They're going to close down the play space because the swings are broken? They can't do that! It's the only safe place for kids to play in for miles! If we all get together maybe we can raise enough money for new swings. Let's tell everyone in the street and see if we can organize a meeting!'

Perhaps the playgroup your child attends has run out of money for new toys; maybe your residents' association wants to plant shrubs in that neglected corner patch; or the local hospital has issued an urgent appeal for incubators. You may have seen heartbreaking images of injured children in a war zone and felt 'Why is this happening? Why can't they stop it? What can I do to help?' Some of you may have raised money for a cause before. Some of you may be inspired to do some fundraising for the first time in your lives.

Whoever you are and whatever the cause, we hope this book will be a valuable aid to your efforts. We have compiled this book for everyone who wants to fundraise – adults and children, men and women, housewives, Scout groups, parent and toddler groups, schools, Rotary Clubs, youth clubs, church groups.

The book draws on the collective experience of hundreds of fundraising groups throughout the whole of England over the last five years. Those of you who wish to read about the local church and fundraising can do so in Chapter 5. Good publicity will be crucial to the success of your fundraising event, which is why we have included a special section about it, Chapter 3.

But what of those who say 'It's all very well raising money for your local playground but it won't solve the problem of a general lack of play spaces'? Indeed, it won't. You may decide that as well as raising money for new swings, you also want to set up a local campaign for more play spaces. The type of fundraising events we describe in this book can never offer an alternative to the provision society needs to make for the education of our children or for care of the elderly, the sick, or the vulnerable. But fundraising events can also raise public awareness and be a learning experience for everyone involved.

'Did you get a leaflet about the fundraising dinner for the special care baby unit? I am going to go, but I'm also going to write a letter to the local paper about the shortage of equipment at the hospital. I think it's a disgrace. Why doesn't someone do something about it?'

Well, you can. This book is for those who think that something should be done and want to do their bit to help.

Even if you think that what we need is a change of Government or local policy or an influx of international resources, you can still do something now to support your cause. This book will give you some ideas about how to do that.

In Chapter 2, we describe the nuts and bolts of how to go about organizing a fundraising event. But before you embark upon the practicalities of fundraising, you will need to assess the challenge that lies ahead and form a plan.

'A hospital scanner? What's that? I thought the Government paid for these things. Why should we have to buy one? Most people don't need them anyway, do they?'

You may be clear about what you are raising money for, but maybe no one else is. Have a think. . . Do people know what you are talking about? Have they ever heard of a scanner? Do they know what it's for? It is always better to assume no knowledge than to imagine everyone knows as much as you do. The chances are, they don't. So explain clearly.

If you are raising money for an existing charity such as

Christian Aid, you will need their permission and they will be able to supply you with all the leaflets you need about the appeal. If you are fundraising for the collapsing local church tower, then you may have to start by writing a leaflet. (You will find more information about how to produce publicity materials in Chapter 3.) If you are organizing a flag day or a door-to-door collection, it is important to make sure that all the people involved are as clear as you are about why you are raising money and what it is for, and that they can answer general questions from the public about it.

If you are setting up a much larger appeal you will have to find out whether you need to register with the Charity Commissioners, and you will have to appoint a treasurer and set up a bank account.

'I'M FAR TOO BUSY TO HAVE A STRATEGY!'

Don't be scared by the word strategy – all it means is working out how you are going to accomplish a task. Say you are going on a camping holiday at the end of the week. You can either wait until the last minute and get into a panic because you haven't got everything you need, or you can sit down with a pen and a piece of paper, write a list and make a plan.

What I need to take:
tent/foam mat/air bed/pump/gas cooker/sleeping bag/wellies/raincoat/jumpers/trousers/money/chequebook/chequecard/camera/film/book/map

What I haven't got or need to buy or borrow:
foam mat/film for camera/raincoat/sleeping bag

What needs to be dry-cleaned or washed:
trousers washed/jumpers dry-cleaned

Plan

Monday:
Ask Julia if I can borrow her foam mat and sleeping bag. Put jumpers in to be dry-cleaned. Can she water my plants?

Tuesday:
If no luck with Julia, go to camping shop and buy foam mat and sleeping bag. Also buy raincoat.

Wednesday:
Collect things from cleaners. Wash other clothes in machine. Buy film for camera. Get book from the library.
Thursday:
Iron dry clothes. Pack. Cancel papers and milk. Give neighbour edible food from fridge.
Friday:
Depart.

We've all forgotten to cancel the milk or found that just as the sun is setting on the mountain we have no film in our camera – but devising a simple strategy should help to cut out the major disasters.

PEOPLE ... TIME ... MONEY

A fundraising strategy is simply a framework involving people, time and money. In Chapter 2 we will go into more detail about how to make best use of the people, time and money you have available, but here are a few things to consider:

People

A fundraising event can involve any number of people. There may be literally thousands taking part in a flag day, house-to-house collection, bike ride or marathon. At the other extreme, you will find in this book a number of events in which only one person takes part – this may be a local celebrity – for example the Bishop of Leicester who climbed the church towers in his diocese, or Father Roy who held a birthday vigil outside his church for one day.

Perhaps there is a well-known figure in your area who can be persuaded to take part in a fundraising event. Or perhaps there is someone with an interesting story to tell, like Pam Richardson, who was recovering from cancer and undertook a marathon walk with her pet dogs. Events which revolve around one person can be very appealing – the event takes on the flavour of a personal passion and it provides a focus for the media.

Even if only one person is taking part in the event, you may need several people to help organize it. If you are concentrating on getting sponsors for your 90-mile hike, who is taking care of the publicity?

We've all forgotten the milk . . .

The main thing to remember about the people you involve in organizing an event is – don't ask too much, don't stretch people too far or they won't want to help you next time!

Time

The next chapter will help you to plan when to organize your event; it will also help you to use the time you have available to best effect. Just as you should avoid asking your helpers to do too much work, or tasks they find difficult, try not to ask people to give more time than they want to.

You cannot always assess the value of an event in terms of time spent organizing it. Some events, like the Smarties appeal, may take a long time to complete but raise relatively small sums of money. Others, like an appeal to help the families of those killed in a disaster, may raise large sums quickly and effortlessly. The publicity around an event can be just as important as the money itself, expecially if it raises the public's awareness of an important issue.

Money

If you want to raise as much money as you can in the shortest possible time, you may find that a carefully worded approach to a few selected individuals may produce the same amount of money as organizing a sponsored swim involving a hundred people.

Always ask yourself the question 'Can we make money or are the costs going to be so great that we may not even end up breaking even?' This seems to be particularly true of large-scale performances, so if you are thinking of staging a concert, BE WARNED. Unless you have managed to get performers to donate their services for free, you may very well get your fingers burnt!

FREEDOM TO THINK

Having a strategy can actually liberate you from worrying constantly that the thing will get off the ground, and can provide space for everyone involved to be more creative. Once you have devised your strategy, you may find that people will feel more secure and come up with more daring ideas!

Everyone can play a part; try not to limit someone to an administrative role. Just because a person offers to take the minutes of your meetings or to make the tea, doesn't mean he/she doesn't have any ideas. Always make sure that you involve everyone, and give everyone a chance to be creative.

It is important not to ask too much of people, but it is equally important not to have low expectations. Sometimes the very best ideas come from the most unexpected quarters – not always from the person who talks his way through the whole meeting! Try to avoid a situation where someone may be feeling 'Why do I always end up having to do all the work?' or 'She never lets anyone else get a word in edgeways'. Above all, a strategy will help you to measure how successful an event has been and help you plan for next time.

AND FINALLY . . .

We hope you will get as much pleasure from the fundraising ideas in this book as we did. There are plenty of useful tips to guide you on your way. There is no shortage of amusing stories and you will no doubt laugh with the contributors as they recall some of the more hilarious moments of their events.

All the ideas in this book are tried and tested. Some of the people who organized them had never been involved in a fundraising activity before. Many of them doubted their own abilities, some of them were nervous on the day, many of them felt they could have done better, but almost all of them will go on to organize other, more successful events in the future. Why don't you join them?

2

How to Go About It

Small, local fundraising events like jumble sales and coffee mornings still provide the bread-and-butter support that many charities rely on. These are not organized by high-flying, professional fundraisers, but by ordinary people. With careful planning, people with little or no experience of fundraising can raise hundreds, even thousands of pounds.

Don't be put off by the technical jargon you sometimes hear when people are discussing fundraising. Everything has its own jargon. You don't have to be an expert to raise money. All you need is some common sense, a good idea and willing helpers.

First you need to choose what kind of fundraising event you want to organize. This will depend on where you live, how many people you think will help, how much money you need to raise and how quickly. Roughly speaking, there are four types of fundraising events:

- *Asking people for money*: this would include street and house-to-house collections and appeals for money by letter or face to face.
- *Commercial ventures*: this simply means making or producing something that people want to pay for. We sometimes buy things because we want to support a certain organization or charity, but more often we want to buy what is on offer because we like it and we want to own it. Take the example of your local charity shop – most people who buy second-hand clothes do so because they want cheap or unusual clothes. The fact that the

shop belongs to a particular charity may be a secondary consideration and may not even be a consideration at all. A successful commercial venture will not need to rely on people wanting to support your cause.

- *Pay-for performances*: concerts, plays, cabarets, Punch and Judy shows – almost anything that involves people paying to see something or be entertained.
- *Sponsored events*: these are probably the most common fundraising events. They involve sponsoring people to accomplish a task, whether long-distance walking, slimming, giving up smoking or keeping quiet for a day.

MAKING YOUR CASE

Whether you are raising money for a summer trip for children from the local school, to repair a hole in the church roof or for a shipment of clothes and medical supplies for the people of Eastern Europe, you need to be absolutely convinced – and be able to convince others – of the need to raise money. Remember that demands for money are being made on people all the time. Bills are daily dropping on the doormat, school uniforms need to be bought, Christmas presents and holidays are an annual expense, little jobs around the house always need doing. On top of all this, there are countless charities knocking on the door, sending out mailings, inviting us to give money to this, that and the other good cause.

You need to be clear about why your cause is important and how the money people give will make a difference. Don't blind people with science. Keep it simple, short and clear.

Imagine you are raising money so that a group of children from the local school can spend a week at a youth hostel in the country. You need to raise £500. How can you make your appeal simple and direct? Have the children ever been to the country before? Perhaps not. So, you are asking people to give so that a group of children who have never been to the country can have a holiday. It will help if you spell out for people just how their contribution will help. For example, if you say that £10 will really make a difference, it will pay for accommodation for one child for one night, they are more likely to pay up.

FORM A GROUP

For most events, you will need a small group or team of people who will take on all the jobs that need to be done. You need people with energy and enthusiasm, possibly people with certain skills. You will need regular meetings, so that everyone knows what they have to do and when they have to do it by. Someone will need to produce minutes of each meeting with action notes in the margin, including the name of who is going to do what.

Helpers may be friends, colleagues, church members or acquaintances. Once you have got together your group of helpers, sit down together and plan your event from beginning to end, making a list of all the jobs that need to be done.

This is your chance to find out about each person's hidden talents. Someone may be good at bookkeeping, another may have a celebrity friend who would make an appearance, another may know someone in catering. Some people like to be in the middle of all the buzz, others prefer to stay in the background. See who wants to volunteer to do what. Does someone need gently persuading that they really are the best person to write the letters? Maybe one member of the group would like a crack at something they have never tried before.

At St Paul's, Wimbledon Park, a musical marathon brought all sorts of previously unrecognized talent out of the woodwork, including that of curate Michael Roden, whose leg-shaking vocals astounded his parishioners.

Just as some people enjoy doing a particularly tricky piece of needlework or writing music, so there are people who craft events. For some, this talent comes naturally; others grow to enjoy the challenge of organizing an event; using the phone, writing begging letters, having to find a clown to replace the one who's just rung in to say she's broken her leg.

Consider the needs of your helpers. It's no good asking Arthur whose wife is ill to come out to regular evening meetings. He wants to be involved but he needs help to care for his wife. Why not have the meetings at his house? Or perhaps another member of the group could offer to stay at Arthur's house while he goes to the meeting.

His leg-shaking vocals astounded his parishioners

Similarly, Jackie may be lacking in confidence about her writing; so don't ask her to do the minutes till she offers herself. Remember that people like praise. Even the smallest effort should be rewarded by a few words of thanks.

Don't bite off more than you can chew. A carefully organized, well-run jumble sale is better than an over-ambitious concert with rows of empty seats.

TIME TO PLAN . . .

You will need time to plan and organize the event, time to organize publicity. Draw up a timetable or schedule. Leave yourself plenty of time to book speakers or celebrities, to book rooms and services. Check that the date you have chosen doesn't clash with other major events in the area.

Some events take longer than others to organize, so make sure you have left yourself enough time to do everything that needs to be done.

How much time you can spend on planning the event will depend largely on the people involved. Would they prefer to work flat out for a short period or at a more leisurely pace for longer? The availability of the people may determine the type of event you decide to hold. Ask yourself the question 'Will we really get everything done in the time available?' Unless the answer is a resounding YES, sit down and think again.

There are certain annual events or anniversaries that lend themselves to fundraising events. The Rev. J. R. Wikeley and two helpers from St Mary's Church, West Derby, made the most of Christmas by organizing a trip to the North Pole for local children to meet Father Christmas. . .

When Charles and Mandy Patterson left their vicarage in the parish of Bures, Suffolk, to move to another parish, they held a Vicarage Closing Down Sale. Some parishes 'beat the bounds' at Rogationtide. What about Harvest Sunday for a barn dance? The May Bank Holiday for a sponsored walk? Check that your event isn't at half term when many people are away. Is the church hall free on the day you want it?

Be realistic about how much time some things take. If you are trying to find some local businesses to cover some of your costs, you will need to allow them time to consult colleagues and committees. Every event will need its own timetable, but here is a sample timetable to give you some idea of the sort of things you will need to consider.

BIGGLESWORTH CRAFT FAIR

Timetable

Three to six months before the event:
- book a hall or venue
- confirm booking in writing
- write to craftspeople in the area asking if they want a stall
- invite a celebrity to open the fair

Two months before the event:
- organize design of posters and leaflets
- arrange printing
- make sure diocesan and parish newsletters have information about the fair (some newsletters have very long deadlines, so check well in advance)
- arrange for catering if necessary
- hire any equipment needed

One month before the event:
- check that all equipment hire has been confirmed in writing
- put up posters and distribute leaflets
- arrange for notices to appear in local press

Two weeks before the event:
- send out news releases
- put up another round of posters
- distribute the rest of the leaflets
- start phoning the media to make sure they have enough information about the fair
- double check that everyone is going to attend

COUNT YOUR COSTS

A careful estimate of the costs involved will ensure that you don't fritter away the money you raise in unnecessary expenditure. Always try to get as many of your costs as possible covered either by voluntary help or by contributions from local businesses.

In St Albans, a cycle ride round the diocese was organized with minimal costs. Publicity material was donated by a sponsor and mailings went out with other diocesan material. All the money raised went to the Church Urban Fund or to specific projects connected to the churches taking part.

Ask yourself 'Are we really going to make money or are the costs so great that we may end up not even breaking even?' Keep alarm bells ringing at the back of your head. Always draw up a budget. Where you are unsure of costs, try to get accurate estimates. Always estimate up rather than down.

BUDGET

You need to prepare a budget – even for the smallest event – and try to stick to it. Make a list of everything that you need to spend, even if you hope to get some goods and services free, or if you intend to seek sponsorship for some of the items.

Sample budget

CRAFT FAIR

Expenditure	£
Hire of hall	100
Van hire	80
Printing of posters	25
Photocopying	15
Tea and coffee	10
Advertisement	35
Contingency	20
TOTAL	£285

Income	£
250 people at 50 pence each	125
Refreshments	120
Sales	350
TOTAL	£595

Estimated net profit £310

The list will include equipment, hall hire, publicity, materials, printing, photocopying, refreshments, transport and petrol, fees, postage and insurance. Shop around and get several estimates for things like printing and van hire. Remember to include VAT in your budget. (This may not be included in your quotes.) Keep accurate records and allow for inflation. Add a little extra for unexpected unforeseen expenses.

Making an estimate of income is much harder. List all possible sources of income – sale of refreshments, entry, raffle-ticket sales. If you are organizing an event for the first time, you may have to consult with previous fundraisers or other organizations to get a rough estimate of how much you are likely to raise.

Try to make your budget work.

SETTING A TARGET

When deciding how much money you want to raise, be realistic. A large sum of money doesn't look nearly so intimidating once it has been broken down into parts, so that people can see how a relatively small gift of time and money contributes to the whole.

Charities that raise very large sums of money for development in Third World countries often focus on one aspect of aid, like medical supplies that people who read their leaflets will see that even £5 will vaccinate a number of children against killer diseases. £5 is a drop in the ocean compared to what's needed, but when broken down in this way, people can see that what they give will make a difference, no matter how little it may be.

Once you have decided how much money you need to raise, you will need to break your target down. For example, how much should you charge for each ticket, or how much does each sponsored walker need to raise?

Who are the people you are asking to give – professional people? parents? residents on a neglected housing estate? rich businessmen? Think carefully how you are going to approach each group. One of the most important rules of fundraising is getting the right person to ask for the right amount in the right way.

WHAT EVENT?

A clear picture of just who you are trying to raise money from will help you to choose the right fundraising event. Jumble sales are popular money-raisers but they provide an important service to the people who go to them – they are a source of cheap clothes. Think hard about who you are trying to raise money from and what is likely to appeal to them. In this book you will find ideas for a large number of events. Whether you organize a Sporting Dinner or a Church Cleaning Day will very much depend on who you want to attend.

Generally speaking, a good fundraising event is something that people will enjoy or get a kick out of, be it a day which offers a challenge of physical endurance, a cheese and wine party, an afternoon with the children or a competition.

If your village fête is well organized and the weather is good, it may be a roaring success. Alternatively, you could end up with a poorly organized washout! You can't do anything about the weather, but you can make sure that you organize the event to the best of your ability.

Here are a few simple guidelines on what makes a good fundraising event. It will:

- capture the imagination
- be appropriate (a £70 per person golf tournament will not go down well in a poor area where most people are unemployed)
- be easy to understand
- be fun
- offer a challenge
- involve effort

SPONSORED ACTIVITIES

Sponsored walks, swims, record breaking, giving up smoking, slimming – you can be sponsored to do or not do almost anything! The principle is simple. You decide to give up smoking and to raise money for your favourite charity at the same time. Ask all your friends, colleagues or neighbours to sponsor you by the hour, day or week. They will agree because they know you (they may think you will never give up) and they will want to support you. They may share your enthusiasm for the charity you have chosen, they may be worried about your health, or both!

Once sponsored walks were all the rage. Now if you want to attract publicity, you may need to be a little more imaginative. Why not try tap-dancing, skating, jiving, singing hymns in a public place or doing magic tricks?

The key to sponsored events is getting as many sponsors as possible. Don't be shy. Ask friends, relations and colleagues. Some people may prefer to give the money in advance. Always have a large sum at the top of the page to encourage generosity. The organizer of a sponsored event should stamp the card of each participant or give them a certificate to verify that they have completed the task. Make sure all the sponsorship money is collected at the end. A sample sponsorship form is on page 18.

INVOLVE LOCAL BUSINESSES

One way of cutting down your costs is to ask local firms to support your event in some way. They may cover all or part of your costs or provide goods and services. Why not have a brainstorm about who can possibly sponsor what, or can offer a service free of charge?

Does anyone on the group know a local businessman or woman, or is anyone on friendly terms with the local restaurateur or printer? Is there someone with a hidden talent – an artist or cartoonist? Does anyone do calligraphy or take good photos? Perhaps the churchwarden or committee secretary has a small local business. Local companies may make a straight donation. Larger companies will no doubt have special budgets for charitable donations. But local branches of major supermarkets and department stores are often empowered by their head offices to make small donations at their own discretion. The best approach is a personal one: send a letter and follow it up with a phone call.

CYCLE ROUND THE SEE 1st MAY, 1989

SPONSORSHIP FORM

I_____, intend to take part in the St. Albans Diocesan sponsored cycle event in aid of
- the diocese's contribution to the Church Urban Fund
- my parish Church (delete if inappropriate)

At least half of what I raise will go to the Church Urban Fund. I should be most grateful for your sponsorship.

I am over 14 years/I am under 14 years but will be accompanied by Mr./Mrs./Miss_____

SPONSOR'S NAME & ADDRESS	AMOUNT per Church	or	per Mile	PAID (date)	TOTAL

All the money raised for the Church Urban Fund, i.e. at least half of what you raise, should be sent to the Church Urban Fund Office, Holywell Lodge, 41 Holywell Hill, St. Albans, AL1 1HE by 30th June, 1989. Cheques should be made payable to the "Church Urban Fund Cycle Round The See Account". Money raised for your Church should be given to your Parish Priest or Church Treasurer.

The Church Urban Fund is a registered charity.

Sponsored by
DEWHURST

Example

Dear Mr Rashid

My wife and I have been regular clients of yours since you opened the Golden Gate restaurant in Billericay. I am writing to ask if you would consider supporting a fund-raising dinner the Billericay Rotary Club is organizing.

As you know, there have recently been devastating floods in Bangladesh which have left countless thousands of men, women and children without homes. We in Britain have our own problems, but these pale into insignificance when compared to the plight of the flood victims of Bangladesh.

Our aim is to raise £5,000 for medical supplies which we hope to ship to Bangladesh within a month. We are approaching several of the most popular restaurants in Billericay to ask if each would provide one course for the meal which we will advertise for £20 per person. We would be pleased to acknowledge your support on all our publicity materials. Perhaps I can call you in a day or two to arrange a time when we could meet and I can give you further details?

Yours sincerely,

Roger Biggs

This event could appeal to the restaurateur because his family may live in Bangladesh. Providing only one course would not be too costly and any restaurant will always welcome free publicity.

If you can get a company director or mayor to say 'I've given £100 to support this vital work', others are more likely to follow. And remember – local businesses want publicity. A local hairdresser may get a lot of much-needed publicity in exchange for a couple of free haircuts.

INTRODUCE A LITTLE FRIENDLY RIVALRY

Why not set targets or incentives for everyone taking part? Ask everyone handing out sponsorship forms to distribute 50 each. Ask each person in the group to sell ten tickets for the concert or 500 raffle tickets. Give a prize to whoever sells the most tickets or brings in the largest number of sponsored walkers. And remember, these prizes can also be free gifts from friendly local sponsors – a candlelit dinner for two at a bistro, two free cinema tickets, a golf lesson by the local hotshot.

BE PRACTICAL

There are certain things that you will need to attend to, however large or small the event that you are organizing – for example safety, access to toilets, refreshments.

Safety

You will always need to spend some time considering the safety aspects of the event. Events involving children should never be held on public roads. If the event is being held indoors, is there a maximum number of people who can safely be accommodated? Are there fire exits and fire extinguishers available? Are there upstairs windows which small children could fall out of? Is there a cooker with hot soup or a scalding tea urn? Is there a front door which needs to be guarded in case small children escape into a busy road? Are there any faulty or exposed electrical wires?

Obviously it is better to spend time trying to avoid accidents, rather than dealing with them after they have occurred. But no matter how careful you are, accidents do happen and it is better to be prepared. Make sure there is easy access to a phone and that a car is always available. Have a First Aid box to hand and, if possible, someone who has been trained in first aid. If you are holding a large event, you may wish to enlist the help of an organization such as St John Ambulance.

Depending on the event, there may be other organizations well placed to help. For example, you will need to contact a Mountain Rescue organization if you are planning a mountain climb, or a Sea Rescue organization for a boating trip at sea.

Make sure that insurance is in order to cover you in case of accident (see Chapter 6).

Where's the loo?

Don't forget that you will need to provide access to toilets, indoor or outdoor, depending on the event. One toilet will not be enough for a do in the church hall that 500 people are attending, especially if it involves drink! Outside toilets can be hired in advance. Make sure they are well signposted and if possible, separate them out for men and women. Provide a baby changing-place if you possibly can and make sure at least one toilet is wheelchair-accessible. Try to provide wheelchair access everywhere, especially to toilets. Ramps are not difficult to organize into most ground-floor buildings.

Refreshments

At a small event such as a jumble sale, you can easily organize a tea stall, preferably with homemade goodies for sale. At a larger event like a street carnival, you may prefer to let local people run stalls for a small fee. There will be times when you will want to provide drinks free of charge, especially to people who are taking part in a run or a jog on a hot day!

When planning an event, work out all the practical details. We cannot provide an exhaustive list as every event will involve different practical tasks, but here is a checklist that will serve as a guide for what you need to do BEFORE THE EVENT. This list does not arrange the tasks in chronological order: it is up to you to decide what needs to be done first, but this list should help as a reminder.

CHECKLIST

- Set a date which you think will get the maximum amount of participation and support.
- Consult the local authority or police for permission.
- Arrange public liability insurance (see Chapter 6).
- Involve as many other organizations as you can – schools, youth clubs, sports clubs.
- Book any venues you will need to use (remember always to check them out first) and confirm booking in writing.
- Choose a safe route. Check it out in detail.
- Plan your publicity (see Chapter 3).
- Plan your administration – sort out entries, sponsorship forms, make sure you have leaflets about your organization.

Where's the loo?

- Arrange for first aid.
- Arrange for outside toilets.
- Approach local companies for sponsorship or prizes.
- Make sure all printed materials will be ready in plenty of time, and book printing.
- Invite local personality to launch the event or take part.
- Arrange all the 'on the day' needs – equipment hire, maps, route marking, stewarding, refreshments, first aid, signposts.
- Send out news releases and phone all the media to make sure they are coming.
- Send out maps of the sponsored walk or maps of how to get there so that no one can claim they couldn't find it!

ON THE DAY

No matter how hard we try, there is usually something that gets forgotten on the day. Those of you who have already been involved in organizing an event will be familiar with the frantic last-minute attempts at signmaking, having to blow up 500 balloons in half an hour or the horrible discovery that no one has organized drinks for the dehydrated runners! There may be very few or a very long list of things to check on the day of the event, depending on how large the event is. You will need to devise your own, but here are some examples of the kinds of things you may include on your list:

- Early morning planning meeting for everyone involved.
- Go through your checklist, making sure everyone knows what to do.
- Brief your stewards.
- Check that all equipment has arrived and tents etc. have been erected.
- Make sure that someone is on the end of a phone in case of any last minute alterations to plans.
- Give everyone membership forms to hand out (if you are a membership organization!).
- Make sure all helpers or 'officials' are easily identified by lapel stickers.

- Issue certificates to all participants indicating how much they achieved, which they can show to sponsors.
- Stewarding is very important at any event involving a large number of people. The last thing you need is for participants to get lost, confused, or irritated by lack of clear direction or information. Roughly speaking, you will need one steward for every ten people attending the event. Stewards should be well informed (you will need to give them instructions before the event begins) and easily identified. Coloured plastic bags tied across the chest or armbands are often used to identify stewards.

AND AFTER . . .

You want to avoid the cry of 'Never again!' from local people who have to clear up your mess after you have gone.

- Make sure you give everyone bin bags to clear up every bit of rubbish.
- Collect all the money and bank it as soon as possible.
- Pay all your bills promptly.
- Thank every one for taking part, those who raised money and all who helped.
- Make a file of names and addresses of everyone who may take part in a future event.
- Chase up uncollected pledges as soon as possible.
- Publicize total collected in the local press and announce next event.
- Hold a party for all the organizers and helpers! Pat one another on the back. What went well? What went wrong? How could it have been done better? Did you raise as much money as you hoped? Why not? What are you going to do next?

3

Publicity

From the time we get up until the time we go to bed, we are
bombarded with news and information. Radio, television,
newspapers, magazines, advertisement hoardings, posters,
leaflets, car stickers, badges, in-store announcements, shop
windows, telephone calls, gossip... We live in a world rich
in news and information. Some of it we seek: we buy our
favourite newspaper or magazine, we tune in to our local
TV programme or radio station. Other times, it seeks us
out: posters on the side of the bus, advertisements on TV,
leaflets left under the wipers when we park the car...

Some of it we need to know or want to know, some of it
we'd rather not know. Occasionally – just occasionally –
we're grateful that someone took the trouble to tell us
something we didn't know already. That's successful publicity.

Good, well thought-out publicity is an essential ingredient in every successful fundraising event. Whether you tell
people individually, give out a notice in church, put up
posters, advertise in the local paper or tie a banner to the
back of a passing aeroplane – your publicity will be the key
to your success. If you want people to get excited and
enthused about your event and what you are raising money
for – you have to make sure they find out about it.

There are a number of reasons why you should spend
time, effort and energy on publicity.

Make or break
First, you want to let people know it's happening. If you
are organizing a garden party, jumble sale or concert –

anything you want people to attend – publicity is crucial. The more people who know about it, the more people will turn up.

You need cakes for a cake stall – but you need customers too. And if you only sell half the seats for the parish panto, you will put in the same effort, but only raise half the money you could be raising!

Good publicity can make or break an event: it can mean the difference between success and failure – between making lots of money, or an embarrassing loss.

Putting you on the map

There are other reasons why you should spend a bit of time (and money) on publicity.

Publicity will help put your church or group on the map. *You* know about the church but does anyone else? A well-publicized event could help you reach people who never knew you existed before. And a good story in the local paper might tell local people something they didn't know before. Maybe the much-loved local landmark will fall down unless everyone rallies round to save it. Or perhaps a picture of the vicar and curate setting off on their sponsored tandem ride will make it clear that you don't just meet for worship on a Sunday but you are raising money for local charities as well.

Good publicity can work wonders for your image! You may be saddled with a Victorian barn for a church – but you can show that beneath its austere, forbidding exterior is a lively, caring and enthusiastic congregation.

A shot in the arm

But publicity can do more than get people to come along – or show that you exist – or tell people about your good cause. It's also important for those organizing and running an event.

Too many things can conspire to make people feel bad about church life. All that talk of sin each week, for a start. And the fact that the church always finds it hard to make ends meet – what with the quota, insurance, vandalism and building repairs. The church is always on the lookout for people to do things – run the choir, the Sunday school, serve on committees. There's no escape at home, either –

From Land's End to John o' Groats . . .

another story on the evening news about falling member-ship in the Church, splits and divisions and that irrepress-ible bishop who doesn't believe in God again!

But *you* know there's more to your church than that. That sponsored abseil by the Venture Scouts down the church tower last week for a start – over £500 raised in one afternoon for flood victims in Bangladesh. What a pity the local paper didn't turn up. So demoralizing. Someone should have told them!

Good publicity can give members of an organization a much-needed boost. Everyone loves reading about them-selves in the local paper. That's why there are so many stories about the Women's Institute, local amateur dra-matics and the schools' sports days. Reading about your event in your local newspaper will make the organizers feel good about the work they've done. And if a charity or local cause has benefited from their efforts, they can justifiably feel proud to have done their bit.

Planning for success

Good publicity doesn't just happen – it's planned. You may be lucky. The ace reporter on your local paper may happen to wander past the church hall just at the very moment the curate's Elvis impression is bringing the house down. But they're much more likely to turn up (with a photographer) if someone invites them in advance.

'AND HERE IS THE NEWS'

You need to have some idea about what is likely to interest your local media. You can then either build up your event to attract publicity – or plan something which you are sure will have a special appeal to your local paper.

Postman attacks Rottweiler . . .

Someone once said that 'news' is something different – something out of the ordinary, something that makes you sit up and take notice. 'Bishop Prays' will not be front page news. 'Bishop Denies Existence Of God' may well be. The media will cover things which are different, surprising or unusual. Most bishops don't run in marathons – or go up in hot air balloons with actresses – or walk the length and breadth of their diocese. Most vicars don't abseil down their church towers – or ride tandems – or row down the Thames. Most choirs don't sing right through the hymn book – and you don't usually get hundreds of Morris Minors all in one place! If it's unusual and different – there's a good chance that your local paper or radio station will want to cover it.

Presenting Bigglesworth's own TV personality . . .

The media love 'personalities' – someone who's famous either because of what they've done or simply who they are. And in a world dominated by the media, those who already appear on it are most likely to appear again!

Two types of 'personalities' may help you attract local publicity.

A national celebrity may be persuaded to open an event or take part in it. Find out who's appearing at the local theatre or taking part in a concert or nearby sporting event. They may well take up your invitation – especially if it's for a charity or local cause. Of course, you will need to invite them in plenty of time, but inviting a celebrity to a 'grand opening' is one way of attracting the media to something which may not at first sight appear very exciting.

Alternatively, you can invite a local celebrity. Fame is, of course, relative. The Archbishop of Canterbury may be of great interest to the national press. A diocesan bishop is likely to be just as famous in his region – and a local head teacher or vicar in their own town. And if you can persuade them to do something a little bit unusual – so much the better. The added attraction of local football players or MPs taking their turn in a sponsored hymnathon may well tip the media scales in your favour.

The oldest, biggest, rarest, and most unusual event in the world!

Is there anything unique about your event? Are you trying to do something in record time? Or for the first time? Or with the most people? Or is it the first time it's ever been done in Bigglesworth?

Every fundraising event is special. But perhaps you are organizing the biggest jumble sale in Bigglesworth, the largest collection of Morris Minors, an unusual book of recipes, the first attempt to wrap St Oswald's in brown paper . . .

The right time – the right place

In today's media world, terrorists and politicians stage events to give the best pictures and gain maximum exposure on the main TV news. You can increase your chances of getting publicity for your event by making sure you time and stage it right. It's no good launching something on Wednesday if the local paper goes to press on Tuesday. If you are looking for live coverage on local radio then you will have to plan it to take place at a time when they broadcast news and local features (usually early and mid morning and late afternoon).

If you want the media to turn up to your event, make it easy for them. Organize a special photo call and press launch at a time to suit them. Or make sure that the Grand Opening and Fancy Dress Parade starts at a time when the local photographer can still get off to cover the cricket match later in the afternoon.

Children and animals

Actors are wary of working with children and animals – they usually steal the scene. You can turn this to your advantage. When the Bishop of Truro walked the Cornish path his labrador, Raya, stole the show! A new church on an out-of-town housing estate was ignored by the press – until the Church Council decided to hold a St Francis Day Pets Service. And a Father Christmas fundraising flight for local children was virtually guaranteed a place on local television. If you can build something photogenic with children or animals into your planning, you are much more likely to get a picture in the paper.

A local angle on a national story

If you want to find out what's, going on in the big wide world, you watch the TV news or read a national paper or listen to the *Today* programme. But if you want to find out what's going on in your town or neighbourhood, you read the local paper or listen to local radio. One way of interesting local media is to give them a local way into a story already featured in the national press.

If you can tie your event into something that's currently in the news, so much the better. Don't simply raise money for Christian Aid – raise it for Christian Aid's latest national appeal, or for medical supplies for the world's current trouble spot.

PLANNING A PUBLICITY CAMPAIGN

Just as a successful fundraising event needs planning and forethought (a strategy, in other words) so does successful publicity. That's why it's a good idea for someone to be responsible for publicity from the outset. And the time to start thinking about publicity is the day you start planning your event – not the day before it takes place. A publicity campaign isn't complicated: it simply means thinking out clearly *what* you are going to do; *when* you will do it; and *how* you will go about it.

Make a list

Make a check list of all the different ways of attracting publicity. Be imaginative and get everyone on the committee to come up with ideas. This is sure to include word of mouth (notices in church, for example), leaflets, posters, advertisements, news releases, articles in local newspapers, items on local radio and regional television. When you have made your list make a note against those which will let people know about the event in advance, and those which will attract publicity on the day.

Be selective

You won't be able to use everything on your check list – you may not have any money for advertisements, for example. Decide which bits of the media you are going to target, bearing in mind:

How much will it cost?

Advertising, printing posters, leafleting every house in the parish, photocopying sponsor forms, sending out news releases – all involve some expense. What free resources do you have available – photocopier? design skills? a printer who may be able to print things at cost? What will you have to pay for? How much of your overall budget have you set aside for publicity? Get some estimates. Be specific. Do you just want someone to print your poster – or are you really asking them to typeset and design it? How much can you do yourself – or ask others on your committee to do? How many posters/leaflets will you be able to use? How many news releases will you send out?

How much time do you have?

The deadline for an organization to receive news about an event may well be much further ahead than you first think. Diocesan newspapers and magazines which come out infrequently may be prepared months in advance; local newspapers, only a week or two. Local area 'What's On' and listings guides vary from place to place but may need the information several weeks or months ahead. Some organizations like to have plenty of warning. Daily TV regional news programmes may look as if they've been put together that morning, but some items may have been prepared several days or even weeks ahead. If you've marked your list with the media you are going to target, find out what their deadlines are and make sure you meet them.

Who is going to help?

Do you have hordes of willing volunteers? Will everyone lend a hand putting leaflets through doors or will you be left to do it all yourself? Who will put the posters up? Where will they go?

Does it fit?

If you are trying to get people to come to your jumble sale or boot fair, a simple leaflet popped through local letter boxes may be much more successful than an advert in the local paper. And a personal letter to parents of the local Scouts and Guides may well be the best way of attracting families to a 'Beating the Bounds' or a sponsored event.

Warm-up events

Can you think of any 'mini-events' which will help draw attention to your main fundraising event? A competition (with a suitable prize) for poster design at your local school or college may not only come up with a wonderful design, but will itself publicize the event. Selling programmes and raffle tickets for the summer fair door to door will not only raise money but let people know that the fair is happening!

You can also set up 'training' events and photo opportunities before a big sponsored event. When the Bishop of Leicester asked the PE department at Loughborough University for advice as he prepared for the London Marathon, he made sure that the local papers knew all about his visit and were there to cover it!

A delicate balance

Try to balance the amount of time, energy and money you will spend on each bit of your campaign with how much you think you will get out of it. Are people really going to turn up to hear the vicar recite the whole of the Bible after seeing an advert in the local paper? Or should you be targeting the congregation specifically? A notice or display in the local sub-post office will reach many of the older people in the neighbourhood, but you will need to find other ways of involving the children.

Talk through your ideas with other people on the committee. There aren't any right and wrong answers. What you decide to do will depend on the event, the resources (human and financial) you have available, who you are trying to attract and how much time you have to do it.

Keep in mind the aims of your event – raising the profile of your group, getting more people to think about how they can help people in the Third World, providing an enjoyable occasion for everyone in the local community. Are you looking for individual sponsors? Do they know about the organization they are being asked to support? Or will they be attracted by the sheer daring and audacity of what you hope to achieve? What individual response do you want people to have to a particular publicity initiative?

FORMING A MEDIA STRATEGY

Timing

You should by now have got a clearer idea about *what* you are trying to achieve through your publicity campaign and *how* you are going to achieve it. You will need to fit your publicity timetable into the main timetable for the event.

You may be looking for publicity ahead of the event to arouse interest. For example, if the vicar and curate are looking for sponsors as they pedal their tandem from Land's End to John o' Groats, then a story and picture in the local paper of them in training for the event (complete with cassocks and dog-collars, of course!) will help to bring it to the attention of those you will be approaching for sponsorship.

You will want to make sure that posters and leaflets are ready in plenty of time. Or you may want to send out a news release shortly before the event so that journalists will not 'bin it' for arriving too soon.

Which media?

Don't put all your eggs in one basket. Use a mix of media. Putting leaflets through the door of local houses may well prove more effective than an eye-catching advert or poster. A complimentary story in the local press will let even more people know that your group is alive and kicking – and may even remind some of those who were thinking of coming that the event is still on! If you use a number of different ways of getting your message across, they will each build on each other. Try to spread things out so that you are not delivering leaflets at the same time as sending out news releases and going to talk to local Scouts and Guides! Be clear about what help you will need and when you will need it. Remember, the more people you have helping you, the easier it will be and the more people will have a special interest in making the event a success!

Don't take on too much. It's better to do a few things well, than plan to leaflet a whole city and realize at the last minute that you are not going to get it done in time.

What are you going to say?

Keep it short. Include the essential ingredients: the event, the time, the place, where to get tickets and further information. Do you want people to know why you are raising money? Keep it simple. Avoid fancy lettering and too much information on posters and leaflets. The same rules apply to news releases. Always let someone else check through you what you write. The closer you are to organizing an event, the more you make take some information for granted. It's far better to let a friend spot a mistake than for 200 posters to reproach you from every tree!

What are your aims?

You are not trying to dazzle people with your brilliance. The aim is to draw attention to your event, to get people to come along, to raise money.

NEWS RELEASES

A news release is probably the single most important tool you have. Newsrooms and editors may receive hundreds each day. A news release is a partially digested piece of news which gives busy editors and journalists all the important facts about a story and tells them clearly where they can get further information. The clearer and more concise it is, the more likely it is to grab attention. It can be used:

- to give advance notice of an event;
- to report on an event that has taken place;
- to give general background information.

If you are looking for publicity, you are most likely to be interested in the first of these.

The five Ws

Every news release should contain the answers to the following questions:

- Who?
- What?
- Where?
- When?
- Why?

You should try to include these in the opening paragraph. (You don't need to have them in that order, just make sure they're all there!)

WHO The First St Oswald's Brownie Pack
WHAT will be holding their first Summer Fair
WHEN on Saturday 5 July, at 10:00 a.m.
WHERE at St Oswald's Church Hall, Stoney Lane, Bigglesworth
WHY to raise over £100 for a new banner and toadstool.

WHO	Winston Green Golf Club
WHAT	will be holding a Celebrity Golf Tournament
WHEN	on Saturday 3 August from 10:30 a.m.
WHERE	at their course off Sandy Lane, Winston
WHY	in aid of St Winston's £1m rebuilding appeal.

WHO	St Paul's, Wimbledon Park
WHAT	will be giving local people a chance to display hidden talents at a sponsored Musical Marathon
WHERE	in the Church Hall, Park Road, Wimbledon
WHEN	on Saturday 1 April from 10:30 a.m.
WHY	to raise money for the Bishop of Wimbledon's Inner City Appeal.

Put the main points in the first sentence.

The First St Oswald's Brownie Pack will be holding their first Summer Fair on Saturday 5 July, *to raise over £100 for a new banner and toadstool.* The Fair starts at 10:00 a.m. at St Oswald's Church Hall, Stoney Lane, Bigglesworth.

Winston Green golf club will be holding a Celebrity Golf Tournament on Saturday 3 August *in aid of St Winston's £1m rebuilding appeal.* The Tournament starts at 10:30 a.m. at their course off Sandy Lane.

St Paul's, Wimbledon Park will be giving local people a chance to display hidden talents at a sponsored Musical Marathon *to raise money for the Bishop of Wimbledon's Inner City Appeal.* The Marathon takes place in the Church Hall, Park Road, on Saturday 1 April and begins at 10:30 a.m.

Once you've got the five Ws firmly set in the first paragraph you can then continue with the rest of the release. Try and include a quote, if possible. It may be easier if you write the quote for whoever is going to be your spokesperson.

Don't forget to

- Put a date at the top.
- Put a title, usually a simple summary of the first sentence.

'LADY MAYOR TO OPEN SUMMER FAIR'
'TV COMEDIAN JACK LADD IN CHARITY GOLF COMPETITION'
'LOCAL CURATE STARS AS ELVIS IN MUSICAL MARATHON'

Leave it to the newspaper's sub-editors to come up with fancy headlines.

- ALWAYS include a day and evening phone number at the end for further information. MAKE SURE THAT SOMEONE IS THERE (it's no good putting down your home number if you are out at work all day. And if a journalist is trying to meet a tight deadline, they won't want to leave a message on an answerphone!).
- Write ENDS at the end of the News Release.
- Draw attention to picture opportunities in a separate note at the end:

Note to Picture Editors: Rev. Michael Roden, complete with Elvis outfit and suede shoes, will take the stage at 11:00 a.m.

Note to Picture Editors: Jack Ladd and the Bishop of Wandsworth will be teeing off at 11:15 a.m.
The winner's cup will be presented at 5:30 p.m.

Other points to bear in mind:
- Check that names are spelt correctly.
- Check you've used people's proper titles.
- Check the time and place.
- Check the contact number at the bottom. Will there be someone to answer the call?
- Avoid jargon and abbreviations. Spell it out. Not CUF but 'Church Urban Fund'. Not PCC but 'Church Council'.
- Use headed paper.
- Use a wordprocessor or typewriter.
- Make sure it's double spaced, that you leave 1 inch (2.5cm) round the edges and don't underline anything.
- One side of A4 should be sufficient. If you need more, perhaps you are saying too much.
- If you must go on to two pages, use only one side of the paper, number the sheets, use the same headline on the second sheet (marked 'continued') and type 'More Follows' at the end of the first sheet.

- Fold the news release contents side out (with the headline showing) i.e. the opposite of a letter. Remember, you are not trying to keep a secret – you want the world to know!
- Get someone else to check it through – preferably someone who knows nothing about the event. They may notice that something vital is missing which you've taken for granted!

SENDING IT OUT

Where

Your check list should already include a full list of all the local newspapers, radio and TV stations. If not, you can find their names in the phone book. If your event covers a larger region, you may want to consult one of the listings publications which may be in your local library. (Ask your librarian which one they stock.)

Send a copy to the News Editor (by title, not name). Address a separate copy to any contact you know by name. If you think your story would make a good picture, send a separate copy to the Picture Editor. (News and Pictures are two completely different departments in most newspapers.) Send a copy to any person or organization named in your release.

When

Timing is important. You need to strike a balance between giving the news organization time enough to prepare a story but not giving them so much warning that they put your release on one side and forget it. Use first class post (it's easier to time its arrival).

Local Press: Daily evening papers go to press about 10:30 or 11:00 a.m. In fact many of the feature pages will be made up at least the day before. Make sure that the news desk receives the release at least 48 hours *before* you want them to use it.

Weekly papers which come out at the end of the week may go to press on Tuesday or Wednesday. They will need to have your release at least two or three days ahead of press day, if they are going to use it.

NEWS from the CHURCH URBAN FUND

Monday 27 March
For immediate release

LOCAL CURATE STARS AS ELVIS IN MUSICAL MARATHON

St Paul's, Wimbledon Park will be giving local people a chance to display hidden talents at a

sponsored Musical Marathon to raise money for the Bishop of Wimbledon's Inner City Appeal.

The marathon takes place at the Church Hall, Park Road, on Saturday 1 April and begins at

10:30 a.m.

One of the highlights of the event will be curate Michael Roden's leg-shaking impression of Elvis

Presley.

'I've been practising in the vestry after Church', said Michael. 'The church is still standing, so I

expect that the Hall will be able to take it!'

The marathon is expected to last all night and is open to anyone who pays £5 to the appeal. The

Bishop's Inner City Appeal is trying to raise £½m from every church in the diocese as a

contribution to the Archbishop's Urban Fund set up to help community projects in needy areas.

ENDS

For further information contact:
Michael Roden, Co-ordinator of the Musical Marathon, on 012 345 6789
or Earnie Cash, Diocesan Co-ordinator of the Bishop's Inner City Appeal, on 023 456 7890.

Note to Picture Editors:
Rev. Michael Roden, complete with Elvis outfit and suede shoes, will take the stage at
11:00 a.m.

PATRON: HM THE QUEEN • REGISTERED OFFICE: 2 GREAT PETER STREET LONDON SW1P 3LX
TELEPHONE: 071-620 0917/8 • FAX: 071-799 1828 • A COMPANY LIMITED BY GUARANTEE
REGISTERED IN CARDIFF NO. 2138994 • REGISTERED CHARITY NUMBER 297483

Winston Green Golf Club
Sandy Bunkers
Winston Green
WS1 234
Tel: 012 345 6789

News Release

Friday 26 July

TV COMEDIAN JACK LADD IN CHARITY GOLF COMPETITION

Comedian Jack Ladd will be among those taking part in Winston Green Golf Club's celebrity golf tournament on Saturday 3 August in aid of St Winston's £1m rebuilding appeal. The tournament begins at 10:30 a.m. at their course off Sandy Lane.

Jack Ladd, star of the TV hit *Funny Faces* is currently appearing in *Babes in the Wood* at the Winston Hippodrome. Others taking part in the tournament include the retired Bishop of Wandsworth, the Rt Rev. C. Crawley.

'We are delighted that Jack is taking part', said organizer and club secretary Fred Tee. 'We have already raised over £500 from competitors alone. We've still got one or two places left if anyone wants to join the famous out on the green!'

Tickets are available at £1 in advance or on the day.

ENDS

For further information please contact Fred Tee, Club Secretary, at Winston Green Golf Club on 012 345 6789 (during office hours) or 012 456 7890.

Note to Picture Editors:

Jack Ladd and the Bishop of Wandsworth will be teeing off at 11:15 a.m.

Monday 30 June

LADY MAYOR AND FORMER BROWNIE TO OPEN SUMMER FAIR

The First St Oswald's Brownie Pack will be holding their first
Summer Fair on Saturday 5 July, to raise over £100 to buy a new
banner and toadstool. The fair starts at 10:00 a.m. at
St Oswald's Church Hall, Stoney Lane, Bigglesworth.

Mayor Vera Important, a former St Oswald's Brownie, will open the
Summer Fair by judging the Grand Fancy Dress Parade.

'I was honoured to be asked to judge the competition', said Mrs
Important. 'It's over 50 years since I was a Brownie. I was
delighted to hear that they're still going strong!'

ENDS

For further information please contact Mrs Maureen Bird,
Brown Owl, on 081 123 4567.

Local television and radio will have a diary file. It may be worth sending it to them a fortnight in advance and following it up with a phone call a few days later. Weekly programmes may be put together quite a few weeks in advance. Send a separate copy clearly marked for the attention of the producer of a particular programme you think may be interested (e.g. the religious magazine, or the morning sequence programme).

Remember: Sending out a news release is a three-stage process:

- writing
- setting it out on the page with all the relevant information
- sending it out to the right person

Pictures

You stand much more chance of getting your story in the paper if you plan a good picture in advance, draw attention to it on the news release and make it easy for the photographer to get the picture when they turn up. Have a good look at the sort of pictures in your local paper. If you have a T-shirt, sweatshirt, logo or badge, make sure that everyone wears it for the photo. You may want to get some T-shirts, caps or posters specially made for the occasion (collect them up and use them again next time!). The bigger and bolder the better (remember the photo may be in black and white, not colour). Follow the general news guidelines above and remember that if you include children you will need their parents' permission for them to be photographed. Above all, let the picture desk know direct – don't rely on the news desk to let them know.

FOLLOW UP

Try to follow up your news release with a phone call at least the day before your event. There are three things to bear in mind.

Timing

Be careful when you call. Call editors and journalists early in the afternoon when they may have a bit more time. If you are sure you've got a good picture, contact the picture desk as well. Find out when your weekly papers go to press (phone and ask them if you are not sure). Again, make a separate call to the picture desk if you think you have a good picture story.

Think, too, about the best time to contact a radio station. Most local radio stations are modest operations with a skeleton staff doing everything! Don't call a radio producer just before, during or immediately after their programme. If you are contacting the news desk remember that they will be busiest just before and during a bulletin (either on the hour or half hour). Most regional TV news programmes have a planning meeting in the morning to decide shooting schedules for that day. Contact them quite early (about 8:00 a.m.) or early afternoon the day before. Make sure you are clear about the date of your event.

Targeting

Newspapers: Ask for the news editor, news desk, picture editor or picture desk. If you already know a journalist or editor ask to speak to them by name.

Radio: Ask to speak to someone on the news desk. If you think your event is the sort of thing covered by a particular programme, ask to speak to the producer of that programme. If they're busy call them back – don't expect them to call you. Again, if you know a journalist, producer or presenter on a particular programme, ask to speak to them by name. If they're busy, ask when you can call them. Don't forget that most BBC local radio stations and many commercial ones still have a religious programme, as well. Make sure you contact its programme producer in plenty of time (at least two weeks before the event).

TV: If you have a particularly unusual and visually attractive event you may be able to interest your regional TV station in covering it on their evening or midday news programme. Ask to speak to the programme editor for the day your event is to take place. If they're busy, ask to speak to someone else working on the programme for that day. Remember, TV will only be interested if you can guarantee good moving pictures (bishop training for marathon, vicar abseiling down tower). Remember that for TV to be interested it's got to be of interest to the whole region – not just your town.

Be brief

Most newspaper and radio staff are trying to do at least six things at once. When you phone, you will probably be the seventh! Keep it short. Ask if they've received your news release. If they haven't, suggest you fax them a copy (marked for their attention by name) or tell them briefly about the event. Ask if they will be able to cover it. Give them your name and phone number if they want to ask any questions. They may not be as enthusiastic about your event as you are. They will make the final decision about whether to cover it; your job is not to try and persuade them against their better judgement, but to make it easy for them to decide whether your event will make a good story. You will be better received (this time and next) if they don't think that you are wasting their time.

Contacting the church press

Don't forget the church press. They may not help you raise money or give you a bigger turn out. But as well as stories of national significance they will sometimes cover events from the parishes. Some denominational papers (*Church Times*, *The Church of England Newspaper* and *Methodist Recorder*, for example) have special sections for what's happening in local churches. Most will be able to use photos taken by the local press. (Most local newspapers will agree to supply them to you if they are suitably credited.) You will find the address and phone numbers of the national church press in the useful addresses section at the back of this book.

Diocesan Communications Officers

Most Anglican dioceses have someone responsible for dealing with the media – Diocesan Communications Officers (DCOs). Their exact role varies from diocese to diocese. Some are full-time but most are part-time and edit diocesan newspapers, are bishop's chaplains, or run a parish as well. Your diocesan office should be able to tell you how to contact them. They may be able to help by sending you a list of media in your area, by suggesting helpful contacts or by giving advice and drafting a news release. If you've got a really astounding story ('Vicar To Mountain Bike To Summit Of Everest'), they should be able to help you contact the national media. At the very least, they will be glad to learn that someone, somewhere, tells them about something before it happens! Make sure that you send them copies of your news release.

Diocesan newspapers

Many dioceses have a newspaper or magazine. Because of difficulties over distribution these may be prepared several weeks or even months in advance. Find out who the editor is. As soon as the date for your event is fixed, contact them direct. Tell them about your plans and ask if they would like something in writing and when you should send it. Find out if they want any pictures after the event, or publicity shots/posters/leaflets beforehand.

News agencies

Many large towns have a news agency which will write material for their local evening paper and try to sell stories to the national press. It may be worth sending them a news release. They should be listed in the Yellow Pages or media listings book in your library. Your DCO should also know who they are. Unless your story is particularly risqué, salacious or astounding ('Vicar Stars In Sponsored Drag Striptease') they probably won't be interested in sending it to the nationals.

Further information

You may be glad when it's all over – and hope that next time an event is planned somebody else volunteers to handle the publicity! But you may discover that it has whetted your media appetite. Your DCO should be able to help you with further reading or training. The Catholic Communications Centre and Church of England Communications Department run training courses for individuals and church groups interested in publicity and the media (see under 'Media' in the Useful Addresses at the end of this book).

A final word

Don't be put off by thinking that the media are a foreign world and should be left to the professionals. Have a go. Good publicity and a successful media strategy do not come in a rarefied moment of divine inspiration, but are largely the result of careful planning and applied common sense.

4

Fundraising Ideas

MEET THE CHALLENGE

Some sponsored events pose a physical challenge to those taking part. This can involve walking, running, jogging or cycling great distances, climbing mountains, abseiling or performing other daredevil feats. Sometimes they require great physical strength or endurance – as in the case of 55-year-old Bill Purchase who ran the whole length of Britain.

Some events are attractive because they offer an adventure combined with a pleasant day out, often in beautiful surroundings. They may involve leisurely walks through picturesque countryside like the Heritage Trek or long and winding journeys by boat like Gently Down the Stream. They are normally outdoor activities, so care must be taken in choosing the right time of year. There can be any number of people seeking sponsorship, from one solitary participant to literally hundreds or even thousands as in the London Marathon.

A larger number of participants does not necessarily mean that more money will be raised. Ian Botham raised an enormous sum for children's charities on his own when he walked from John o' Groats to Land's End. The key to raising money in any sponsored event is getting a large number of sponsors and this is usually achieved by organizing good publicity well in advance.

Gently Down the Stream

A week-long, sponsored 126-mile row of the Thames from its highest navigable point at Lechlade in Gloucester to Teddington Lock in London.

Amount raised: £1,200.

Rev. Tom Merry, Holy Trinity, Stroud:

'It all began with a chance remark. A craftsman in our parish called Roger Davies commented that he would like the challenge of building a rowing boat in 48 hours. I said if Roger could build a wooden boat in 48 hours, then I would sail it down the River Thames. Roger made the boat as part of a craft exhibition we were holding to celebrate our church's 150th anniversary. In the end, Roger and his two children and another family decided they would like to take part and Roger built two more boats.

'We chose a week in August, hoping the weather would be fine. Then we contacted parishes along the route asking them if they could provide us with a place to pitch our tents. We had to apply to the Thames Water Authority to get a licence for the three boats.

'People in the parish sponsored us, including some commercial firms. We also raised money *en route* by taking a bucket round while we were waiting in the locks and two or three churches handed over cheques. The only money we had to spend was on licences for the boats and food for the journey. We were very lucky in being given a free loan of camping equipment from the local Red Cross and we borrowed some things from the local Roman Catholic school.

'Central Television filmed the launch at Lechlade. We also got coverage in some of the national papers, on the local media and in the church press. The media liked the fact that the boats were homemade and children were taking part. They also focused on me being a vicar. The headlines were hilarious: "Pushing Out The Boat", "Rev Rows His Boat Ashore", "Oar The Merrier", "Quay To Church Cash"!

'Unfortunately Bishop Gibbs's wife fell into the river at the launch! *En route* we broke an oar and magically Roger was able to fix it. On another occasion a fish jumped into one of the boats. Everyone took part in rowing, even the children. Most of us had blistered hands and one of us had blisters elsewhere! But all in all it was a perfect adventure.'

After the boat's successful voyage it was put on sale to raise more funds. Photographs and equipment used on the journey, the map and day logbook were put on display in a local hall.

Editors' note This event shows how a chance remark can lead to a big adventure! People who can build a boat by hand are few and far between, but every parish has its share of talented people who may be willing to help out with your fundraising event. Perhaps the most important lesson to learn from the Merrys is the fact that they didn't stop fundraising even after the event was over. It would be all too easy to sit back after such an achievement and put your feet up. You would certainly deserve it. But by going that extra mile and organizing the sale of the boat, the family were able to raise even more money.

Land's End to John o' Groats

A sponsored run from Land's End to John o' Groats (844 miles) over a six-week period.

Amount raised: £5,000.

Bill Purchase, Fakenham:

'I did the run in August when I was able to take six weeks off work. It took 40 days and 40 nights, running some 25 miles a day. A local church committee of four people organized accommodation, sponsorship and backup. I trained for about four months before the trip, running 20 miles a day.

'The Bishop of Norwich wrote to every parish in the diocese suggesting that people sponsor me for a penny a mile. I was sponsored by people throughout the Norwich diocese and churches on the route raised money for their own appeals.

'There were a few costs – evening meals and some of the accommodation, met by the diocese. Press releases were sent to radio stations *en route* and I was interviewed by many of them. I think they were impressed by the scale of the run and the fact that I was doing it 'the hard way' – I had next to no backup, only a driver who was also a church organist. (Remember Ian Botham's huge backup team.)

'The worst moment was when I fell flat on my face and sat shivering alone and bleeding by the roadside. But the wonderful people I met and the money I raised made it all worthwhile.'

Editors' note The most remarkable thing about this event was the fact that Bill Purchase was undertaking such a great physical challenge at an age when most people are content to mow their lawns. A personal letter from the Bishop of Norwich asking for support from every parish in the diocese undoubtedly made a difference. Anyone who is proposing to take on such a great test of physical endurance ought to consult their doctor at the outset. In addition, even the fittest person will need to spend a considerable amount of time in training before the event begins.

The Heritage Trek

A 20-mile trek through the picturesque Hebden Valleys. Walkers came from 200 parishes in the Wakefield diocese. Over 350 people took part.

Amount raised: £8,000.

Ron Carbutt, Bishop's Centenary Fund, Wakefield:

'The Trek was on a Saturday during an August Bank Holiday weekend. The Mountain Rescue Team, St John Ambulance, the National Trust and the Countryside Commission Rangers were all involved. The brochure and walk details were taken from a tourist publication – we just adapted it for our own use! The trek is tough – 20 miles through rugged countryside – but it captures the spirit of challenge and adventure. The walkers see it as a fun day out for the family – raising money is a worthwhile added advantage.

'Fundraising needs to be imaginative and innovative to get people interested. Our experience is that people will respond to an event which presents such a challenge. Despite the fact that the route was described step by step and markers had been out since first light to guide people through the difficult stages, some people still managed to get lost! In the end, everyone was accounted for, but not all on the official route!'

Editors' note The bulk of the work in devising the route was saved by using an existing walk. This is an excellent idea as it saves an enormous amount of work beforehand when every step of the route has to be checked for possible dangers or dead ends. But if you do use a route which has already been mapped out, do make sure that you get the necessary permission before you adapt it for your own use! If you make it clear in your initial approach that you intend to give publicity to the local tourist board on all your materials they will be more likely to agree. You don't have to live near spectacular countryside to organize a sponsored walk. For those who live in cities, the route could have some historic or architectural interest.

Bishop's Cornish Coastal Walk

Sponsored walk round the Cornish coast (265 miles) over three weeks, by the Bishop of St Germans, Rt Rev. John Richard Llewellin. A large number of people joined in, making this a major Cornish event.

Amount raised: £31,542.

Rev. Mary Coney, Truro:

'Two of us prospected the route in detail beforehand; there was a local contact person in most coastal parishes who organized support locally. Some local National Trust wardens were very helpful and arranged free parking and agreed to be on standby in case of accidents. I also asked each local town if there were any major events which might overlap.

'I obtained local authority licences for street collections all the way round, but I had no previous experience in some of the finer details.' (See section on collections, Chapter 6.)

'We had great media coverage – Bishop Richard's progress was featured in daily bulletins on Radio Cornwall. As far as the media is concerned, you have to be co-operative, polite and not too pushy. They like humour and any quirky story. Bishop Richard had his labrador Raya with him most of the time which helped a lot!

'Be aware that if you are not going to be on the spot, it is difficult to enforce safety precautions and to comply with local authority and police recommendations. Volunteers are not always sufficiently aware of safety! In fact we had no accidents through the grace of God! I think the most important consideration of church fundraising is that money is not the overriding consideration. It's no good raising money while causing offence or putting people's lives at risk. Raising money goes to some people's heads like strong drink!'

Editors' note The Bishop was extremely fortunate to have someone as well organized as Mary Coney to organize this event. You can just imagine the tragedy that would arise if someone were to fall over a cliff into the sea. It is important to maintain a sense of fun throughout, but only once you are completely satisfied that every safety precaution has been taken.

PILGRIMAGES AND JOURNEYS WITH A THEME

A pilgrimage is a journey with a special meaning. A pilgrimage can be as simple as a 'Beating the Bounds' or a sponsored bike ride around the perimeter of your diocese, as long as the route or destination has meaning for you. If you are organizing a pilgrimage, make sure that everyone taking part has some information about why you have chosen this particular route or what the historical significance of your event is. The media may be especially attracted by a pilgrimage, but make sure you are able to describe why the pilgrimage you have chosen has special importance for you.

Inner-City Pilgrimage
A sponsored walk round inner-city churches in the Southwark diocese. Twelve of the churches had already featured in a fundraising calendar. Around 500 people took part.

Amount raised: £15,000.

Bernard Day, Shirley St John:

'Walkers were attracted mainly by a desire to see inside the churches. We wrote to every parish in the diocese asking for exhibitions to be put up in the churches, for volunteer stewards to direct walkers near difficult junctions and to give drinks to the walkers. On the day, churches put on a wonderful variety of events – exhibitions, fêtes, bell-ringing, guided tours, giant chess games, music recitals and craft fairs. One church offered walkers coffee and jellied eels!

'The general consensus was that it was a good idea, well

organized and thoroughly enjoyable – even if some were a little footsore at the end.'

Editors' note This is a good but simple idea which can be used in any diocese. What a wonderful incentive to walkers to know that there will be a different event in every church they visit. One of the attractions of this event is that local people are involved in organizing the exhibitions. This brings people into the church and helps create fun and enjoyment which has positive spin-offs for all the churches involved.

Cycle Round the See
A diocese-wide cycling event in the Bedfordshire and Hertfordshire countryside. Sixty churches and hundreds of people took part.

Amount raised: £10,000 to the diocese and £10,000 to participating churches.

Mrs Hardie, diocesan office, St Albans:
'We chose three interlocking routes, covering the north, south and middle of the diocese. One of the organizers personally cycled the three circuits – each 70 miles long – and visited every church taking part. We liaised with the police to avoid traffic congestion. Every participant was sent route information and copies of Ordnance Survey maps of the routes. Participants cycled round one or more of the routes, calling at designated churches, where their cards were marked.

'When the sponsorship money came in, participants were sent a certificate signed by the Bishop, showing how much they had raised and thanking them for the effort.

'The event was widely publicized partly because of its scale and because it was on a Bank Holiday when newspapers are looking for stories. Also, the publicity materials were of a very high quality. It involved an enormous amount of hard work. Every aspect was meticulously planned. In the end, it was a huge success.'

Editors' note It helps to send out brief accompanying notes with information about things like toilets, refreshments, pubs and any other useful information. Always try to avoid busy roads.

The idea of sending a personal note from the Bishop, thanking everyone for their efforts, was an excellent one. Each person will feel valued and will be more likely to take part in the next fundraising event.

Mitres and Minors

A convoy of approximately 35 Morris Minors driving round the perimeter of the Blackburn diocese. There were 500 spectators and 300 participants including two bishops.

Amount raised: £800.

Derek Hartley, St James's, Blackburn:

'The convoy set off at 6 a.m. and finished at approximately 9:30 p.m., having travelled about 280 miles. People from the church and members of the Morris Minor Owners' Club took part. We spent £100 on producing commemorative plaques and commercial sponsorship covered the cost of our posters.

'On the day, the parishes were so generous that the whole party was full to bursting with food and drink, which was laid on spontaneously and eaten out of a sense of duty and courtesy. If I were to organize a similar event in the future, I would go on a diet beforehand!'

Editors' note This event got a lot of publicity, mainly because of the novelty value – everyone loves Morris Minors! The fact that two bishops were taking part was an enormous boost. The image of a bishop driving off in a convoy of Morris Minors was irresistible to local newspapers. In an event like this, you will attract Morris Minor fanatics as well as people who want to support your charity. It is often a good idea to incorporate something that will attract a lot of people on its own merit as well as people who want to support you.

Bishop's Progress

A series of twelve sponsored walks by the Bishop of Lincoln, Rt Rev. Robert Hardy, in the diocese. The walks were designed to cover as much of the diocese as possible and people from each deanery were invited to accompany the Bishop.

Amount raised: £12,000.

Bishop of Lincoln:

'I usually led these walks and spent my time walking up and down, talking to the people taking part, who came from all walks of life, young and old. Attendance varied from about 20 to well over 100. The walks were organized by deaneries and had support from two diocesan co-ordinators.

'A schedule of my walks was sent out in advance, containing the day and time of the walks, routes and destinations. There was also a blank sponsorship form with me amusingly depicted in a cartoon! We enclosed an extract from the Highway Code, a draft press release, instructions to walkers and a short description of what the Bishop's Progress was all about. Most important of all was a detailed breakdown of how exactly to organize every aspect of the walks – safety precautions, toilet arrangements, transport, backup support, publicity, refreshments and social gatherings.

'After each deanery organizer had deducted any essential expenses, the balance was forwarded to the diocesan office. Each deanery was then credited with 25 per cent of the gross proceeds.

'At one of the church services, my dog Sam lay down to have a sleep under the pews and slept the whole way through. At the Blessing at the end he woke up and started barking loudly. Everyone was very amused and it brought to an end a very happy afternoon.'

Editors' note The key to the success of this event was the detailed instructions on how to organize every aspect of the walks which were sent to each deanery in advance. The fact that the pack included a draft press release ensured good publicity at local level. Many events of this kind can be broken down to parish or deanery level. With one or two central organizers and a good pack of instructions, you can achieve remarkable results.

'Moving Church' Pilgrimage

A 17-mile sponsored walk, run or jog from the bomb-site of a church to its new site at Biggin Hill. Forty people took part.

Amount raised: £4,000.

Eric Heselwood, St Mark's, Rochester:

'All Saints is a recycled church – it was bombed and then moved brick by brick to be rebuilt on a new site. We organized the sponsored run on the 30th anniversary of the beginning of the move. We planned the run along exactly the same route the church had travelled piece by piece.

'I had just come to the parish and I felt we had to do something imaginative and I wanted to encourage our small congregation to raise money for the Fund. Because our church is nationally known, we were able to get good local publicity. There is now an old people's home at the site of the old church. We went there for the send-off and while we were there we showed the residents pictures from our archives. It was a wonderful day.'

Editors' note This was a lovely event which attracted a great deal of media attention locally. The media were undoubtedly attracted by the send-off when the organizers showed archive photographs to the elderly people in the old people's home.

Perhaps there is something in your parish or diocese which has historical value that could be incorporated into a fundraising event. Reconstructing a historical event will always attract a lot of publicity, and there are all sorts of ways in which you can get pictures in the local press. Could you dress up for the occasion? Could you use a horse-drawn cart or even a local steam train? Who is the oldest person in the parish? Do they remember when the event actually happened?

The Lambeth Walk

A sponsored walk over nine days from Wakefield Cathedral to a Garden Party in aid of the Church Urban Fund which was being held at Lambeth Palace – a distance of 232 miles.

Amount raised: £15,000.

Stan Evans, former Bishop's Fund Director, Wakefield:

'This was a symbolic link from north to south. The Church Urban Fund is a wonderful way of bringing the reality of deprivation to the forefront.

'I organized the walk myself, using the network of parish link officers to drum up support. Church members across the diocese organized events to support the walk. Around 3,000 were involved. We used posters, a letter from the Bishop, the diocesan newsletter and press releases to local press to publicize the walk.

'Our costs were roughly £500 for fuel and subsistence, which was deducted from the funds raised. We got sponsorship for the support vehicle and we had hospitality *en route* from the clergy, who offered meals and free overnight stays. We had to get police clearance for the walk and insurance for the back-up caravanette.

'One day, we decided to put the flush portable loo outside the caravanette while we were having lunch and we left it in a layby. When Les, my support driver, went back to retrieve it, a man was putting it into his car boot. He said he was taking it to a local police station, but Les reclaimed it and we continued on our way!'

Editors' note Not everyone would feel it was necessary to take a portable loo on a sponsored walk! However if you do, don't leave it behind! This event had the support of a famous cricketer who attended the send-off and attracted a lot of media attention. The sending out of press releases to local press all along the route attracted quite a lot of local publicity.

Pilgrimage to Glastonbury
A pilgrimage on foot from Walsingham to Glastonbury, with three dogs Lyng, Bullet and Pippa.

Amount raised: £400.

Pam Richardson, Plympton St Maurice:

'First and foremost, my pilgrimages are acts of worship, a witness to my faith. Raising funds is of secondary importance. Nevertheless, the people I encounter like to acknowledge my efforts and give money and accommodation as well as love and prayers.

'June 1989 saw myself and my three faithful companions Bullet, Lyng and Pippa take the first steps of a 242-mile walk to Glastonbury from Walsingham. My first visit to Glastonbury was in June 1987 when I became aware that all was not well with my health.' (Pam has had two cancer operations.) 'I made a vow that if my health was spared, I would walk to Glastonbury as a religious exercise – it just seemed the right thing to do.

'I collected money at home, *en route* and in church. I kept a logbook and took photographs. I have been lucky enough to have completed five pilgrimages. I have no backup, no car behind me. My only backup is God, discipline and my dogs.'

Editors' note This pilgrimage was an extraordinary personal achievement by a woman who had fought off a potentially life-threatening illness. The fact that Pam was accompanied by three dogs will have attracted a great deal of local publicity. The media is very fond of using stories about people who demonstrate outstanding courage in this way. We are a little surprised that the national press did not get hold of this story.

MARATHONS AND VIGILS

A marathon can involve any activity carried out over a longer period than usual. Unlike the Non-Stop Bible-Read below, it need not continue until the participants are ready to drop! However it must be unusual or long enough to attract some publicity. When planning a marathon, it is important to make sure that all participants are fully aware of how their health may be affected by the event. This is especially true of anyone with a history of ill-health or anyone who has a disability. In a marathon, money is raised through sponsorship, or by giving a lump sum on completion of the task. Where the task being attempted breaks new ground, try, as in Model Marathon below, to go for an entry in the *Guinness Book of Records*.

Father Roy's Birthday Vigil
An all-day vigil by a vicar outside his church on his birthday, to receive gifts for the Church Urban Fund.

Amount raised: £400.

Rev. Roy Large, Bishop's Tachbrook:

'I wanted to raise money and I thought a personal touch would give extra appeal. I arranged my birthday vigil informally with the help of a few individuals. It was mainly passers-by who contributed although some people had seen our posters and had driven over specially. We didn't incur any costs as everything was done voluntarily and no one charged for their services.

'All my meals, including breakfast, were brought to me. It was a cold, sometimes wet day and a surprising number of people offered the vicar a little bottle of brandy! One local biker jumped off his motorbike, dropped a note onto the collection plate and rode quickly off. I don't think he wanted to be seen!

'My true age has still never been revealed.'

Editors' note What a charming and simple idea! This could be replicated in every parish, vicar willing. The attraction of the event is that it doesn't involve undue suffering and it is actually quite a pleasant way to spend the day. The local press would be interested in taking the vicar's picture, especially if some good-hearted soul were to bring him a birthday cake at some point.

Just a Minute . . . Marathon Talk-In

A twelve-hour talk by a vicar on subjects suggested by congregation. The vicar was sponsored per hour and some of the audience were sponsored to listen! About 100 people attended.

Amount raised: £1,200.

Rev. David Lowman, Wickford and Runwell Team Ministry:

'I sat in a chair in church and spoke on subjects submitted by the congregation for twelve hours non-stop, except for a short break each hour for a drink and the loo. I stipulated that subjects could be theological, political or humorous.

'I publicized the talk by using posters and leaflets and through the local press. On the day, I got national coverage. The only expenses were on throat lozenges and Lucozade!

The local press might be interested . . . if some kindly soul were to bring him a cake . . .

'The event took place in November and several people brought their Christmas cards and wrote them. By 9 p.m. I didn't want to stop. I had no trouble dreaming up things to talk about. Even the local undertakers donated £50.'

Editors' note Here is another example of something completely simple, yet so unusual that it is bound to attract a lot of publicity. This event proves that if an idea is unusual enough even the national media will cover it. Obviously it helps if your vicar is amusing and a good story-teller. An event like this costs nothing and provides endless amusement and fun for everyone involved; why not repeat it every year?

Non-Stop Bible-Read

A Bible-reading session over 70 hours from Genesis to Romans 8 at a lectern outside Worcester Cathedral. One man took part – and survived to tell the tale!

Amount raised: £3,800.

Neville Andrews, St John the Baptist, Beckford:

'I began the Bible reading at 6 a.m. on a Monday and gave up due to double vision at 3.30 a.m. the following Thursday. This was over a late spring Bank Holiday when there was good weather and short hours of darkness. About twelve people supported me, including my wife, and several hundred people came to watch. My wife and a helper brought me sustenance and provided lighting at night.

'As I was intending to stand at a lectern outside Worcester Cathedral, I had to get permission from the Cathedral and I informed the police. The only costs were food and stationery. I wrote to several hundred people enclosing a sponsorship form and we produced leaflets to hand out. I got local newspaper and radio coverage and I was on BBC Midlands television.

'In addition to the five-minute break I had every hour, I kept my throat lubricated every ten minutes or so with a sip of orange squash. By mid-afternoon on the first day my tongue began to swell. On the third night the man who was there to keep me awake kept falling asleep and I had to arouse him continually. Towards the end I fell asleep standing up and had great difficulty in seeing the words on the page.

'In the end I read out more than 90 per cent of the Bible and as far as I know, no one has ever read the whole thing aloud. I was 57 at the time of the Bible-read and I won't repeat it. I wish a younger person who wishes to do this every success!'

Editors' note Perhaps the reason no one has ever read the whole of the Bible aloud is because they would die first! On a more serious note, this event illustrates how an amusing idea can turn into a nightmare. If you are considering a marathon of some kind, it is important to think it through, to take into account your age and your health, and in some cases to consult a doctor. In the end, Neville Andrews was suffering from severe sleep deprivation and although he raised a lot of money and survived to tell the tale, we really wouldn't advise anyone to attempt this.

Model Marathon

A competition to guess how long two Hornby model trains and two Scalextric cars would run non-stop. One car broke the existing record and appeared in the *Guinness Book of Records* in 1991 and 1992.

Amount raised: £2,000.

Rev. Bryan Apps, All Saints, Bournemouth:

'There were lots of tasks – building tracks, testing models, keeping non-stop watch for the first 72 hours and then every six hours night and day. We sent entry forms to every diocese to distribute to every parish.

'We launched the competition at Jaguar in Coventry with Sir John Egan posing with the actual Le Mans winning car and a British Rail area manager started the race. We had coverage on BBC television, ITV, Sky, Radio Solent, the *Church Times* and local papers.

'Hornby supplied the models and tracks and IBM provided the timing equipment which had to meet Guinness Record standards. The Chase Manhattan Bank met the cost of 50,000 entry forms. We offered four prizes of complete train and car sets, each valued at about £100, to the four people to make the most accurate guess. The entry fee was 25p per estimate and each form allowed for 16 estimates.

'The Scalextric Jaguar ran non-stop for 1,771.2 miles over a period of 866 hours 44 minutes 54 seconds. After the competition we held an auction to sell off the surplus model equipment and Johnnie Dumfries donated the driving suit he wore when he won the 1988 Le Mans 24-hour race in a Jaguar.'

Editors' note This competition was organized in such a professional manner that it is surprising that it didn't raise more money. 50,000 sponsorship forms were sent out and there was an enormous amount of publicity. However, prior to the event, most of the publicity was local and it is doubtful that a large number of sponsors were found from other parts of the country. Note that all the equipment was provided by the companies concerned. It was a nice touch to ask a celebrity racing driver to donate his suit for auction!

Another marathon sent in to us was a hymnathon – a non-stop sing of every hymn in *Hymns Ancient and Modern,* which raised £750. This was organized by D. Hartley of Mitres and Minors fame, who wrote: 'This was an act of worship and opportunities for evangelism were seized during the late hours of the night with drunks or other inquisitive persons!' His advice to anyone wishing to organize a similar event: 'The next time, I would choose a livelier hymn-book (and a shorter one), and I would have a fuller supply of throat lozenges.'

SALES AND AUCTIONS

AUCTIONS

An auctioneer is a key figure in any auction, so try to enlist the help of a talented one. It may be worthwhile to pay him or her if you cannot get the service free. So important is the role of auctioneer, that holding an auction should depend on whether there is one available or not. Some time must be spent assembling items and cataloguing them. With antiques and other valuable items, you may need expert advice on valuation.

Remember to show the items for at least a day before the auction, and supply all viewers with a catalogue which lists each lot number. It is not normal practice to charge admission, although you may charge a little for the catalogue. You raise money at an auction by agreeing a percentage with the person who gave you the item. This is of course negotiable and people may well be moved by the spirit of generosity and donate all of the money raised to your cause.

Grand Auction

An auction of goods donated through parishes in the deanery. 200 people attended.

Amount raised: £14,688.

Rev. Christopher Atkinson, Cartmel:

'We asked each parish to appoint a representative. Each was asked to find not less than 20 lots, which would give us a total of 400 lots. A professional auctioneer agreed to give his services free, although his staff would be paid. In fact, several of them only took a part of what they earned. The auction was run on entirely professional lines.

'In the end, we finished up with 488 lots. On top of this, the general quality of the goods made it obvious we would easily reach our target. The lots varied from a sack of potatoes to a few fine antiques! Everything went without a hitch – we even made a profit from the sale of refreshments. Our original target had been £5,000. The final profit was in excess of £14,600!

'We had one remarkable contribution – "The Fairy Caravan". From the beginning we knew it was of considerable value but we never expected it to be worth £4,600! Our expenses were only 5 per cent of the amount realized. Nearly all the money raised came from non-church people. The average amount raised per lot was £21. This was an excellent fundraising event – it brought people together, small parishes felt encouraged to join in, a lot of information was disseminated, it made a lot of money painlessly AND it was enjoyable!'

Editors' note The idea of appointing a representative in each parish and instructing each representative to bring in not less than 20 lots was crucial. Each representative must have felt the need to come up with 20 decent lots. This was a manageable amount for each parish representative. It is not unlikely that each one was able to approach people he or she knew quite well to ask them to contribute something. Obviously the quality of goods donated is a reflection of the area. There are places where you would be unlikely to find an antique that no one had realized was worth more than £4,000!

Another auction, the Church Urban Fund Charity Auction, raised over £3,000 and attracted about 400 people in Liverpool.

Again, one person from each parish was asked to collect items. An agent printed and distributed catalogues through the trade (at his own expense) and acted as auctioneer on the day free of charge. The local authority offered the civic hall at charity rates and provided a caretaker. The Bishop of Liverpool (Rt Rev. David Sheppard) and his wife gave a set of Mason ironstone jugs which attracted the highest bid in the auction!

Auction of Promises

Alun Glyn Jones of St Mary's, Twickenham wrote to us about an auction of promises he successfully organized. This is an auction where people offer to provide services to the highest bidder. Mr Jones says they chose this event because 'our aim was to raise a large sum of money in one evening so that we could avoid having to organize lots of small fundraising events'.

They succeeded – 220 people came and they raised £4,000 in two hours. The promises included the use of holiday cottages, meals, baby-sitting, plane tickets, gardening and decorating.

The event was organized by a committee of five people who undertook the following tasks: preparing the auction leaflet, publicity, finance, refreshments and organizing the evening itself. Costs were publicity, refreshments and postage but they were all covered by the entry ticket.

SALES

When organizing a sale, remember to take into account the time needed to collect the material (jumble, antiques, junk) or to make it (crafts, cakes, jam). You may need to leave a long period to assemble non-perishables and organize a drop-in session the day before for perishable goods to be delivered. Virtually anything can be sold. You should always ask your contributors how much they think the item is worth. Take into account what your customers can afford, how much time and effort has gone into making the item and its commercial value. And remember, everyone wants a bargain.

Nearly new or good-as-new sales are now subject to consumer protection legislation relating to unsatisfactory goods. You can get advice about this from the Local Authority Health Department.

Giant Sale

An auction of furniture, garden tools, bikes and household goods.

Amount raised: £1,500.

Ron Carbutt, Cawthorne Parish Church:

'We hold a Giant Sale annually in our parish as it is such a good fundraiser. It started off some years ago as an Attic Sale on the village green – we now take anything and auction it off in the parish hall.

'Because we are perceived to be an affluent village, a small advert in the local press brings in a good crowd and the market traders. Everything is sold – second-hand toilets, patio doors and broken chairs.

'Good prior publicity is essential. Getting people to clear out attics and garages takes a little push, but it is remarkable what is uncovered. On the day itself, crowds turn up just to see what is on offer. There is no fuss, no numbering of lots, we simply offer individual items for sale – if no one bids, we just add something else to give it a value.

'The whole thing takes up only one Saturday afternoon – it is fun, lively and without risk. So far, every single item has been sold.'

Editors' note This event speaks for itself – bargain appeal, curiosity, fun, good fundraiser, easy to organize. When people organize a fundraising event every year, it is usually a winner.

Christmas Pudding Sale

The annual sale of mixed (but unsteamed) Christmas pudding by pound weight.

Amount raised: £200 each year for four years.

Virginia Greany, Hessle:

'This is a good community, seasonal event. It is fun and can yield 100 per cent profit. The following three points are very important:

- undersell good quality local supermarkets;
- have a cheap source of microwaveable basins;
- use vegetarian fat and free-range eggs (to corner health food market).

'The tasks involved are buying and storing dried goods, supervising the mix, sales, orders and publicity.

'We organized our initial publicity mix in church after parish Eucharist on 'Stir Up Sunday' (next before Advent). We used posters and the parish magazine, the diocesan paper and pulpit nagging to publicize the event.

'We used snob appeal by saying the puddings were by appointment to His Grace the Archbishop of York, who has bought his Christmas puddings this way for four years. This really was a great help. And we got the vicar to bless the mixture with an ad hoc liturgy.

'All our profits came from pudding eaters and from selling off the plastic dustbins by auction. We sold the puddings at £1.20 per lb but the wet mixture is good and heavy. The only costs are the raw materials and the mixing bins. The church funds carried a slight risk whilst the stuff awaited mixing!

'One year we used baby baths to mix the ingredients, thereafter huge plastic dustbins. The local press are more than happy to come and take pictures of the great 'stir up'. As I have five children and a very busy life I would recommend an organizing committee to help.

Christmas pudding

Ingredients

1lb Fresh white breadcrumbs
1lb plain flour
1 level teaspoon salt
2 lbs raisins
2 lbs currants
1 lb sultanas
1½ lbs HARD Vegetable fat
12½ oz almonds (without skins)
1-2 nutmegs, grated

1 tablespoon mixed spice
1lb dark brown sugar
1lb candied peel
Grated rind and juice of 2 lemons
1lb eggs (weighed in their shells)
1 wine glass rum or brandy
1 small teacup milk
½ pint brown ale, stout or Barley wine
2 large carrots, grated.

Method

Into an enormous bowl (baby bath if doubling recipe) put everything EXCEPT eggs, milk, ale/wine, carrots and lemon juice. Then beat the eggs, add to the mixture with the four remaining ingredients to give a dropping consistency.

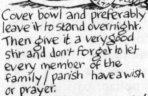

Cover bowl and preferably leave it to stand overnight. Then give it a very good stir and don't forget to let every member of the family / parish have a wish or prayer.

When mixed, treat as any other pudding giving it a longer than usual steam for a really dark colour. Wrap in greaseproof paper, not foil for the first layer anyway, or renew the greaseproof paper lid and keep in basin until required.

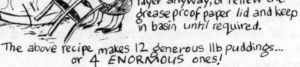

The above recipe makes 12 generous 1lb puddings...
or 4 ENORMOUS ones!

'The event creates a feeling of fun just before Christmas. This really is a star quality fundraising project.'

Editors' note We would recommend this event to anyone. Depending on where you live, you may be able to charge a little more for the Christmas pudding mixture, in order to increase your profit margin. Why not give it a try this Christmas? The recipe is on the preceding page.

Vicarage Closing-Down Sale

A sale of items surplus to requirements on sale of vicarage. The house was full of old junk which had accumulated over many years. 200 people came.

Amount raised: £1,800.

Mandy Patterson, Bures:

'This attracted a lot of people who had a sentimental interest in the vicarage and in our departure.

'We put posters up around the village and advertised in the parish magazine. We purposely did not advertise in the press as we wanted it to be a very local event. The only costs were about £2 for photocopying but a great deal of effort was involved over a few days in assembling, pricing and arranging items for sale.

'We priced things fairly low and people spent generously. They queued up to buy old Sunday-School chairs they had sat on as children. An old bath we had used as a sheep dip eventually went for 50 pence and was carted off down the drive on someone's head. A triumphant parishioner beat a dealer to the vicar's father's riding boots, much to the dealer's chagrin!

'We had to be very tough with all the dealers who heard about the sale on the grapevine and we needed all the help we could get from a retired dealer from the village who came to help. There were literally queues of people waiting for us to open. The whole thing was great fun and now many people in the village have a bargain memento from a much-loved house.'

Editors' note It is ideal to combine a sale with an event that will attract people in itself. In this case, many people may have turned up out of curiosity and ended up carting something down the lane! There is an insatiable demand for old and antique furniture and bric-à-brac, not to mention church pews, which seem to adorn the kitchens of many a middle-class household!

FAIRS AND FESTIVALS

You can either organize and staff a fair yourself, in which case you will need a large number of helpers to run stalls, or you can book a hall, organize the publicity and let stalls to other organizations.

Here are a few ideas for stalls for fairs and festivals: Homemade cakes, jams and pickles, Children's face painting, Jumble, Second-hand books, Guess the weight of the cake/lamb, Tombola, Toys, Plants, Horse or donkey ride, Balloon race, Coconut shy, Handicrafts, Fortune-teller, Punch and Judy, Bouncy castle.

Skeleton Fair

What, you may ask, is a Skeleton Fair? This unique event has all the positive financial results of a massive fair, but with the hassles TOTALLY removed!

Amount raised: £1,025.

Rev. Andrew Warner, St Nicolas's, Great Bookham:

'No one spends hours of committee work organizing the Skeleton Fair. You do not need to hire or borrow any equipment whatsoever. It is impossible for weather to spoil it – even earthquakes and snow. There is no chance of spilling ice-cream down your dress, getting hit by a stray coconut, or your child getting lost in the crowd. You will not be asked to look out a load of posh junk to fill a stall. You do not even have to give up your precious weekend to support it!

'A few weeks before the date of the Skeleton Fair, send out a form like the one overleaf:

'Ask everyone to sit down and fill in the form, then, having added up what you would have spent, come along to the church on the day and donate that sum. No hassle, no junk, no frayed nerves, the whole of the rest of the weekend free and the knowledge that you have done something tremendously valuable and important!'

```
┌─────────────────────────────────────────────────────┐
│                   SKELETON FAIR                      │
│  If I had attended a Grand Church Fair, I would      │
│  probably have spent the following (for myself and all│
│  my family):                                         │
│                                      £         p     │
│       Entry:                                         │
│       Programme:                                     │
│       Raffles:                                       │
│       Ice-cream/candy-floss/etc.                     │
│       White elephant stall:                          │
│       Coconut shy:                                   │
│       Bowling for the Pig:                           │
│       Plant stall:                                   │
│       Cake stall:                                    │
│       Bottle stall:                                  │
│       Roll-a-Penny                                   │
│       Wheel of fortune                               │
│       Hot dogs                                       │
│       TEA tent                                       │
│       BEER tent                                      │
│       CAR PARK                                       │
│       Other stalls                                   │
│  EITHER                                              │
│       Petrol to/from event                           │
│  OR                                                  │
│       Bus/Train fares                                │
│       Thank offering for not                         │
│       being asked to serve                           │
│       on the Committee:         _____            │
│  GRAND TOTAL                    £____:_____          │
│                                                      │
│                  Contributed by:                     │
└─────────────────────────────────────────────────────┘
```

Editors' note This idea has great novelty value. It would work best when used as one of a number of fundraising activities. If a skeleton fair were to be your only annual event, you could be accused of laziness! However the opportunity to take part in the skeleton fair would come as a welcome relief to those who have already had their fill of sponsored walks, danceathons and pie-eating contests.

Cathedral Carnival

This was a carnival of stalls and sideshows in Gloucester Cathedral precinct, preceded by a procession of floats round the city, attended by about 300 people. Proceeds were kept by parishes. Rev. Fred Carroll, Cheltenham, Gloucester was the main organizer: 'Each parish decided the nature of the stall or show but it had to be on a theme relevant to the Church Urban Fund. There was a roundabout, swingboats and a bouncing castle for the children. For the procession we had to have a police escort. The posters and leaflets were printed free of charge by the students at a local college as part of their training. The floats were judged by the Mayor and a local supermarket gave bars of chocolate to the people on the winning float!'

EXHIBITIONS AND OPEN DAYS

Publicity is crucial to the success of exhibitions and open days because the amount of money you raise depends on how many people turn up on the day. This means striking posters prominently displayed and possibly advertising in local papers. As well as charging admission, you can charge for a small catalogue and sell tea, coffee and cakes. In some cases like the 'Precious Ceramic Boxes' below, items may be sold. In others, like 'Spring into Action', people are attracted in droves by the exhibit.

Exhibition of Precious Ceramic Boxes

An 'at home' exhibition and sale of ceramics and hand-made cards, by ceramic artist Kate Gardner. More than 200 attended.

Amount raised: £180.

Kate Gardner, St Luke's, Duston:

'Some people don't like going to galleries and the home is

a great, welcoming place. We asked some friends to help us set up the exhibition the night before and I provided a meal and wine. We ate and drank while putting it all together and had a great laugh. We held the exhibition over a period of two days (Friday and Saturday) near Christmas and our neighbours did tea and coffee.

'We sent out invitations, mostly to friends, who came from all over the diocese. There was a live phone link on local radio on the morning the exhibition opened and we had photos in all the local papers. The costs were tea and coffee, ceramics and cards. Two-thirds of the money raised went towards costs – the materials and the firing of a kiln.

'I would suggest to anyone doing something similar just to stick to Saturday with a long opening time, say 9 a.m.–6 p.m., to allow people who work to drop in.'

Editors' note This event did not raise large sums of money although it attracted widespread publicity. Perhaps the single most important thing about it was the fact that the artist invited people into her home and made them welcome while at the same time exhibiting her work for sale. It was as much a social event (and a very successful one) as anything else.

'Spring into Action'

A farm open day at lambing time for people to view new-born lambs and their mothers. More than 250 people attended.

Amount raised: £300.

Andrew and Carol Vellacott, Capel St Mary:

'We held the viewing on a Sunday afternoon in early April. Four helpers took entrance money and the church youth group helped with the teas. It obviously attracted a lot of children. All our publicity was given free – a free advertisement in the local paper and the local school circulated our publicity materials.

'Lambs are popular for all ages. We had no costs at all. All that's needed for an event of this sort is time and patience – especially by the sheep!'

Editors' note Unlike most other people, farmers have a

natural asset that people are willing to pay to come and see. In any event like this, it is better to keep the organization simple, which keeps costs down and gives a better net result.

Open Gardens Scheme
Members of Gloucester National Gardens Scheme were invited to have a special opening, or to donate a part of their usual proceeds for one year. About 30 garden owners took part.

Amount raised: £2–3,000 over two years.

Susan Beck, Cirencester:

'The idea came to me because our garden was featured in a book *The English Vicarage Garden*. I knew that Gloucestershire had a wealth of lovely gardens, so I obtained permission to write to fellow members of the National Gardens Scheme in the county.

'Gardening is very popular in this part of the country. We hoped part of the appeal of our scheme would be that of rich natural beauty helping to raise money for deprivation and poverty. I wrote to local radio and TV and produced a poster and booklet. My only costs were duplicating the booklet. After my initial letters to some 230 National Gardens Scheme garden owners, I received a cheque for £500 from someone who was unable to take part.

'I must confess to being slightly disappointed with the amount raised. Although Gloucestershire appears to be a wealthy county, those who do support their churches are often beset by repairs to ancient buildings.'

Editors' note Anyone wishing to organize a similar event would need to consult the National Gardens Scheme, as they have strict rules covering the donation of money to other charities. It is also worth bearing in mind that garden owners are receiving more and more requests to hold special openings from different national and local charities.

Vintage and Classic Car Rally
A rally of vintage and pre-war cars by local owners. The day of events included a local Treasure Hunt, a car display, driving tests and children's activities. Around 80 people took part and 400 attended.

Amount raised: £1,600.

Rev. George Perera, St James's, Maghull:

'At the outset we split the organizing into six tasks: dealing with cars and entry, organizing the Treasure Hunt, supervising the site, catering, children's rides and music in the church.

'We publicized the rally in classic car magazines as well as all the usual channels. We had to get permission from the police and from the RAC for the Treasure Hunt. We produced a guide for sale on the day which described the cars in four categories – vintage and pre-war, post-war, motor cycles and vehicles of special interest. These included a Reliant 'Ever-Ready', a Morgan Replica and the Leyland Tiger.

'The entry charge for people bringing in cars was done on a donation basis and a lot of money was raised on the gate. We also had children's rides and stalls with automobile jumble! Our costs were £400 but almost all of this was met by private sponsorship. The only disaster was the weather – it rained all day – but despite that, most people seemed to enjoy themselves.'

Editors' note Car rallies and exhibitions are very popular, particularly in country areas where more people have cars. If you are organizing an event involving cars, it is better to get in touch with the RAC to ask them for advice. At an event like this one, where only adults can take part, it is always best to arrange some kind of entertainment for the children so that families can participate. Better still, try to arrange for a crèche or someone to be in charge of a bouncy castle or adventure playground, so that parents will be free to enjoy themselves!

COMPETITIONS

The main attraction of entering a competition is the prize. The more exciting the prize, the more people are likely to enter. See if you can get a free holiday weekend from your local travel agent or hotelier, a candle-lit dinner for two in a local restaurant, a hamper of goodies from a delicatessen, two tickets to the latest theatrical performance. Many theatre or restaurant owners will be happy to comply, provided you offer to give them good publicity.

Here are a few ideas for competitions: Balloon race, Bed/pram race, Beetle drive, Bulb/flower/vegetable-growing, Darts, Donkey derby, Fishing/golf tournament, Talent contest.

Volcano Night

Competition to build the longest-lasting 'volcano' – made of sand with a fire on top – on the beach. The last fire to be extinguished by the incoming tide was the winner. Around 30 people took part and many more came to watch.

Amount raised: £600.

Rev. Wilf Curtis, Filey:

'If you live near the sea, this is very easy to organize. Choose a time when high tide is between 7 p.m. and 8 p.m. You must site the volcanoes roughly where the water will be just before high tide. Start building in a straight line about an hour before high tide and STOP when the tide is about five metres away from the volcanoes. No further maintenance is required!

'People of all ages joined in. We had teams of children and teenagers with only one adult per team. We had to notify the Coast Guard and the police about our plans. We organized a collection from spectators and participants and we sold a hot supper of soup and hot dogs afterwards. We had no costs as the teams provided their own spades and materials for firewood, paper and coal.

'The event created so much excitement. And on the night the press turned up. There was great cheering and tears as individual volcanoes collapsed. We had so much fun.'

Editors' note This is sure to attract the media because it is such an unusual and visually attractive event. Because the event takes place at night and there are so many fires, you have to take great care of all the children involved. There may be a limit to how much money you can raise in an event of this kind, but it is so much fun, it is bound to attract people to your cause. For any event that takes place

The Great Canterbury Duck Race

on the beach, make sure that you notify the relevant authorities – coastguards etc.

The Great Canterbury Duck Race

A race of plastic ducks on the river with riverside events. Around 4,000 people took part in the race and another 2,000 watched.

Amount raised: £5,000.

Tessa Till, Canterbury:

'There were 4,000 ducks bought for £1 each. Every duck had a number. The race was started from a bridge in the city by five organizers tipping the ducks into the river from sacks. The river took them approximately half a mile through the city to the finishing post.

'We had stalls, barbecues and all sorts of games on the grass alongside the course of the race. We publicized it on local radio, in the local papers, through posters, loud-speakers, with a sandwich-board man and a town crier! We also heavily promoted the race in schools and through the parish magazine. The only permission we sought in advance was from the local authority.

'The only problem was that it rained all day! The event was quite hard work but was deemed a success and it is being imitated by others. The ducks can of course be sold used and unused!'

Editors' note If you are going to buy as many as 4,000 plastic ducks, it would obviously be sensible to try to strike a good deal with a manufacturer or department store. They may agree to give you a hefty discount if you offer to give them publicity. They may be attracted by the idea that the whole town is going to take part. An event like this would benefit from having a celebrity to tip the ducks into the river. It doesn't need to be a national figure, just someone famous in the locality.

Amateur Golf Tournament

A golf tournament for teams of two with prizes for each member of the first five teams in the main tournament and the first three individuals in a putting competition.

Amount raised: £2,000.

Margaret Pantrey, St Martin's, Dorking:

'We had to organize this on a day when we could have use of the local golf club. None of the main organizers played golf, but we had help from friends who advised us step by step and on the day itself. We charged each team of two players £70 and we provided coffee and biscuits on arrival and lunch afterwards.

'The tournament was organized with both scores counting – players using $^3/_4$ of their handicap. (We asked for proof of handicap.) The putting competition went on all day for individuals. We had to pay for publicity and all but £15 of the entrance fee went to the golf club for the lunch and use of the facilities.

'The event was so successful that the five of us have been asked to organize a similar tournament for another charity.'

Editors' note For an event like this, it probably helps to be on friendly terms with the local golf club. Why stick to golf? Both tennis and bowls would make excellent summer tournaments.

Bread-making Competition

A demonstration by a master baker. There was also a bread-making competition where people brought their loaves to be judged on the evening.

Amount raised: £128.

Rev. Susan Hardwick, Chilvers Coton:

'The Master Baker was well known locally. As well as his baking skills, he was also very, very funny. People gave money at the door if they wished. We also auctioned the bread – both by the baker and competitors. Around 70 people attended.

'The baker used one loaf as an example of how one should not make bread – this turned out to be the vicar's entry. The only costs we incurred were on printing posters, which was absorbed into the church budget. Despite the fact that many of the entries prided themselves on their ability to cook, the first and second prizes went to two brothers, aged seven and ten.'

Editors' note This really is a lovely event and you don't need a master baker – you could invite anyone who is known locally for his or her ability to make good bread or cakes. The same type of event could also be organized for wine-making, beer-making, floral arrangements, Christmas decorations or virtually anything you can get people to have a go at trying to make themselves.

BON APPETIT!

Everyone who enjoys eating can be lured into attending an event that involves a meal. It is important to pitch the price of the meal at those likely to attend and to provide value for money. An important ingredient in any meal is the company. Some people will be attracted by the possibility of meeting a local or national celebrity. Make it special by taking advantage of the time of year or by having a theme or special menu – Christmas or Thanksgiving dinner, Chinese or Indian food, Elizabethan or Medieval Banquet, Barbecue.

Sporting Dinner

A formal dinner for sportsmen and women with speeches from sports stars and raffles.

Amount raised: £2,500.

Tom Moffat, Padgate:

'This was a black-tie event at a local hotel which provided a three-course dinner. We didn't need a special licence for alcohol as the hotel had one.

'The hotel charged about £11 or £12 per person per meal, but the participants paid about £20 per ticket for the event. There was a group reduction for a table of ten i.e. £150 instead of £200.

'The participants were approached through personal contact (a promotional letter to recommended people) plus some advertising in the diocesan newspaper. We had a raffle and auctions and we approached local football clubs to donate prizes for the raffle. On the night, we had a former professional footballer, a rugby international player and the Bishop of Liverpool, David Sheppard – a former Test cricketer!'

Editors' note This event could be organized almost anywhere where there are sporting activities. The great advantage of such an event is that there are groups of people you can easily target to attend – rugby, cricket or tennis clubs in particular. If you don't have any national or international sports stars near you, don't worry. Locally known heroes and heroines of the sports field will do just as well. Obviously you need to charge what people are able to afford, depending on where you live.

The Movable Feast

A progressive meal involving about 50 people, which is at the same time a good fundraiser and a very enjoyable evening.

Tessa Till, Canterbury:

'You need an organizing committee of about four people who are willing to do some cooking. Pick an evening a few weeks hence (probably a Saturday) and send invitations to 40 or 50 people – you can each invite ten friends – to a wonderful meal in good company for about £10 a head.

'Each of the organizers has to cook a three-course meal – starter, main course, sweet and coffee – for about ten people. The guests are sent a personal code number consisting of three digits. Each digit represents the home of one of the people supplying the meal. The guest also receives a map detailing names and addresses of hosts, each one with a number. The guests will arrive at house number one at 7 p.m., where they will eat their first course, house number two at 8 p.m. for the second course and house number three for the dessert and coffee at 9 p.m. At the end you can all get together and listen to talk about the organization you are raising money for.

'Depending on what people can afford, you can charge anything you like and make the meal accordingly. At our movable feast, everyone enjoyed moving from house to house and spending time with a different group of people, although at first the men were a little wary. As you would expect, the women were wonderful organizers, they were very enthusiastic and did all the cooking. And on the night, the men enjoyed themselves thoroughly!'

Editors' note You don't need to be Delia Smith to take part in this event – you just need to be able to produce a simple, edible meal. Bear in mind that quite a few people are either vegetarians or semi-vegetarians – they eat only fish or white meat. Sometimes it's easier just to cook a vegetarian meal for everyone! This event is thoroughly enjoyable for everyone involved – except perhaps, the dishwasher.

Shrove Tuesday Pancake Party

A pancake party involving a fancy dress parade or cabaret. Pancakes made by men!

Elizabeth Hale, the Vicarage, Lacey Green:

'I have run these parties in three parishes and the policy has always been that the men cook and serve the pancakes. As many have never cooked a pancake in their lives, the results are many and varied. You will find that a happy camaraderie develops and not a little competition over the look and quality of the finished product!

'The format is very simple. Beg or borrow large quantities of eggs, milk, flour, sugar and lemons and ask the cooks to bring their own frying pans. In one parish we borrowed camping stoves so that we could cook six pancakes at once. The first part of the sessions (about two hours) is devoted to eating. Then you can have a fancy-dress parade, with judges and small prizes for the children, then 45 minutes of organized games for adults and children. These parties are really very popular.'

Editors' note Depending on where you live, you may be able to get people to cough up about £5 each, but if you have to buy all the ingredients, your net profit may not be very great. Perhaps you could persuade a local farm to provide eggs or you could ask everyone to contribute some ingredients or a filling for the pancakes.

PAY-FOR PERFORMANCES

At concerts, plays or pantomimes, most of the money raised comes from the audience, so it is important that the performance is of a high quality or has strong local appeal. Publicity is crucial to ensure a full house and it is worth producing attractive posters and displaying them prominently throughout the area well in advance. Is there a well-known performer in your area who may be persuaded to take part in a concert? Or is the local band a big enough attraction?

Some very unusual performances can attract a large audience. For example, Rev. Arnold Bennet from Heckfield raised £440 at a memorial lecture for Neville Chamberlain on the 50th anniversary of Munich. The lecture went down very well locally because Chamberlain had a local connection – he spent his last days at Highfield Park in Heckfield and now his ashes are interred in the Abbey.

Another unusual performance which raised £1,000 was a one-man reading of highlights of *Summoned by Bells*, the autobiography of the late Poet Laureate Sir John Betjeman, in Blackburn Cathedral. Michael McFall, who organized the evening, said, 'The performance was a sell-out success. Everyone was enthralled. You could tell! Nobody coughed from beginning to end.' Perhaps there is something special that could be organized in your parish.

PUBLICATIONS AND RECORDS

When you embark upon a commercial venture you are entering the marketplace alongside local businesses and you can make substantial profits if you market your goods properly. On the other hand, poorly packaged and badly promoted goods will stay on the shelf gathering dust.

If you are producing a book or a recording, the first thing to establish is: who will want to buy it? Once you have satisfied yourself that there is a market, your task is then to publicize the book as aggressively as you can. This applies to everything you produce for sale. Many people are afraid of entering into the commercial world, but use any contacts you have in business for advice, and take heart from Tessa Till, below, who raised £50,000 by selling *The Bishops' Cookbook* from her own kitchen table.

Bishop's Brew
An anthology of clerical humour compiled by Ronald Brown, Bishop of Birkenhead. The book has been reprinted three times.

Amount raised: 'Several thousand pounds'.

'On a visit to New York, the Archbishop of Canterbury was asked by a journalist – "Archbishop, do you intend to visit any nightclubs in New York?" "Are there any night-clubs in New York?" countered the Archbishop. The next day the papers reported that the first thing the Arch-bishop of Canterbury asked on his arrival was "Are there any nightclubs in New York?" '

The Bishop of Birkenhead:

'Having turned down suggestions that I should swim the Mersey (with all the pollution, it would have been easier to walk over), or jump out of an aeroplane (I trust they meant with a parachute), I hit upon the idea of a book of jokes. Jesus had a sense of humour but most people don't see it because they are Jewish jokes.

'Most of the jokes came from Cheshire clergymen. *Bishop's Brew* was first published in 1989. It was reprinted three times and spent six months on the best-selling list. Sadly, the joke was on me. Before I received a single penny in royalties, the firm went into liquidation. Happily, the paper-back version had to be reprinted within a few weeks of its appearance.

'Here is one of my favourites: The vicar's small daughter was burying a dead bird in the garden: "In the name of the Father, and of the Son, and into the hole he goes. Amen." '

Editors' note To relaunch the *Bishop's Brew* in November 1991, the Church Urban Fund organized a photocall in London which involved the Bishops of Birkenhead, Chester and Stockport reading excerpts from the book. The photograph appeared in *The Daily Telegraph* the following day. *Bishop's Brew*, published by Arthur James Limited, Cranbourne Road, London N10, is still selling well, with proceeds going to the Church Urban Fund.

Bishops' Cookbook
A book of recipes from bishops and their wives who attended the 1988 Lambeth Conference. Profits to Church Urban Fund and Christian Aid.

Amount raised: over £50,000.

Tessa Till, Canterbury:

'I got about 100 recipes – mainly from the wives of the bishops who had attended the Conference. I simply hijacked everyone in sight to help. Someone volunteered to type, local restaurants sponsored the first print run, my husband and son drew illustrations, a nun friend did the calligraphy, my son's godmother drew a parrot and family and friends did the layout.

'As for marketing – I badgered people. I kept phoning. I kept visiting. I sold £20 worth in the street in London in two minutes. I didn't spend much. Sponsorship for the initial print run was about £700. Packaging – well, the local supermarket is quite used to me saying "May I have some of the stuff you wrap bananas in?" (bubble wrap) and carting mountains home. And the local bookseller supplied boxes and padding.

'The retail price of the book was £2.50 and we only dealt with a minimum of ten copies. The wholesale price was £1.75, so 75 pence was being made on each copy.

'Orders, packaging and postage were performed on the kitchen table. Not everyone wants a book, so I had a tea cloth designed, using some of the material in the book.'

Editors' note Because bishops and their wives from all over the world contributed to the book, it was possible to drum up a lot of regional publicity. To launch the book, bishops and their wives donned aprons and cooked their recipes for regional television and the press. There was also a lot of coverage in the national papers, as the cookery correspondents were delighted with the book.

Releasing a Record – Loud Symbols
The release of *Loud Symbols*, an album on LP, cassette and CD by A Geoff Mann Band.

Amount raised: £2,000.

Geoff Mann, St Luke's, Deeplish:

'The idea of a benefit album came to me when Church Urban Fund Week was called "Light in the City" and supporters put candles in their windows. To me, that represented a power cut, which is not what the kingdom of God is all about.

'The music of A Geoff Mann Band could be described as heavy funk, progressive jazz pop. People are called to all sorts of things according to the gifts they have been given. I got a lot of support from the Bishop of Manchester and from Food for Thought records.

'The record didn't cost anything as the record company Music for Nations (of which Food for Thought is one label) funded it fully. The record was released as a project in its own right. The Bishop of Manchester was at the end of one song repeatedly asking "Why should the devil have all the best tunes?" (a question first put by his great-grandfather General William Booth).

'We promoted the record through a week-long tour of clubs, pubs and the odd church, and there was a lot of media coverage – an interview on Radio 1, national press coverage and satellite TV. Lots of audiences seemed to think I was some kind of cabaret act in my cassock.'

Editors' note Unlike recording a cassette of church music and selling it, producing a record is altogether a more complicated business and can only be undertaken by those who are in the business. However that is a different matter from trying to persuade a performer to donate some of his or her royalties to your cause. There are a few singers who have already made their sympathies public. Bear in mind that some issues can become 'flavour of the month' – e.g. the environment. You can write to anyone, no matter how famous, for support, but you are probably better off sticking to people who you know or suspect are sympathetic.

Loud Symbols was released in April 1990. It was available in record shops as well as from the charity. If one person in each parish had bought a copy, we would have made at least £20,000. However the idea did not catch on with the church-going public whose musical tastes may not have been catholic enough to embrace A Geoff Mann Band!

Sally Army on Cassette
Rev. Fred Carroll of Cheltenham made a cassette of hymns sung by the local Salvation Army Band. The proceeds, after paying all expenses, were £690, purely from sales. Two large stores agreed to take a limited number for sale – and each sold out. The costs, including the cost of production, inlay

cards, padded envelopes for the cassettes, posters and post-age on mail orders, came to £590. The Salvation Army gave their services free of charge, as did a soloist who sang on the cassette. In all, 500 cassettes were sold.

Church Music Recording
Another successful recording which raised £1,500 was a collection of music sung by Holy Trinity Choir in Guildford. *English Anthems* features twelve English anthems recorded in Holy Trinity Church in September 1990. The cassette was produced by Herald AV Publications, The Studio, 29 Alfred Road, Farnham, Surrey GU9 8ND. More than 600 copies have been sold.

Festival Software Services
Rev. David Johnson of Holy Trinity, Idle, in the Bradford diocese raised almost £2,000 for the Fund by developing and marketing an original computer programme at a cost of just £100. The original programme enabled millions of Amstrad personal computer users to index their computer files. People from all over the world bought copies. They formed a limited company to market the products – Book-vine Ltd, trading as Festival Software Services. David John-son says: 'We had high advertising costs and the advertisements were not always productive. If I were to do this again, I would definitely get someone with commercial expertise to help us market the product.'

Diocesan 15-Month Calendar
A full-colour, quality 15-month calendar depicting life in each of fifteen deaneries.

Amount raised: £10,000.

R. Williamson, St Mary's Newchurch in Pendle:

'We asked each of 15 deaneries to provide artwork depict-ing life in their deanery. There was a good and very varied response. One professional artist sent in a painting, one was a cartoon and the rest were done by amateurs. One painting was done by a seven-year-old child.

'The calendar sold for £2 and cost about £1 to produce (a big printer gave us a 10 per cent discount).

'We had the calendars packaged and delivered to one

central point, then we got a sponsor to pay for the calendars to be transported to all the deaneries. They in turn distributed them to the parishes where they were sold in the churches. Some local shops and post offices sold them.

'We were over-optimistic in the number we thought we could sell. If we were to do this again, we would aim to sell about 70 per parish. We were told by the printer that a 15-month calendar was unique and many people loved the unusual format.'

Editors' note This highly unusual idea raised a relatively large sum of money and unlike most calendars, all the artwork was done free. This is relatively simple to organize, perhaps the most difficult task being after the calendar has been produced, the distribution and marketing of the product. Nothing has been said here about publicity. A well-planned publicity campaign would be essential to ensure good sales.

COLLECTIONS, APPEALS AND TAXES

Collections are subject to certain legal requirements which you need to be aware of (see Chapter 6). If you are collecting house to house, you need to map out the area, giving each collector about 100 houses. Each collector needs to wear a badge and must have identification and a permit as well as a collecting tin.

When making an appeal, you must communicate clearly what the money is for and it helps to give a breakdown, e.g. £5 will buy one blanket for a homeless person. Some people disagree with this approach, but in pure fundraising terms it has proved to be successful. Always record and acknowledge every donation and keep a list of names and addresses which may be used in the future. If you are making an appeal by post, it is better to include reply paid envelopes.

To ensure the security in the Mile of Coins collection below, you will need plenty of helpers. Alternatively you can remove the coins each time you cover one metre and replace them with a line of chalk.

Smarties Appeal

A campaign to get people to eat tubes of Smarties and then fill up the tubes with 20-pence pieces. Roughly 100 people took part.

Amount raised: £900.

Jack Roe, Anlaby St Peter:

'We launched our Smarties appeal at the Christmas Eve service when children and parents were there and the church was full. We also chose this service to attract people who were not already familiar with the Church Urban Fund.

'The attraction of a Smarties appeal is its simplicity, and you only have to give 20 pence at a time. Rowntree in York donated 100 tubes of Smarties the first year. The following year we raised the same amount of money although we had to buy the Smarties for about £20.' (How mean! (Ed.))

'One Smartie tube holds 65 20-pence pieces – £13. We asked people to fill the tubes over a period of a year, making a target of £1,300. About two-thirds of the tubes were returned both years.

'At the Christmas Eve service in 1990, one man took two tubes. It turned out he was visiting from his home in Buckinghamshire, but thought it a good idea and wanted to take part. The following Christmas he sent me a cheque.'

Editors' note Using the Christmas service to involve as many children as possible is a good idea, but we feel that a year is a bit too long to keep up the momentum. Over a year, people are bound to forget, move away, get caught up in other things or lose their Smarties tube! We would suggest a date not more than about three months hence, preferably when people are coming together at a special church service or other event.

Church Cleaning Day

The 'non-participation' tax was used to accomplish a complete spring clean of a parish church – and raise money at the same time!

Amount raised: £20.

Mrs Gwen Ingram, St Francis of Assisi, Strood:

'We chose the nearest Saturday to Patronal Festival which

Church members of all ages from two upwards took part . . .

was wedding-free. The vicar organized the cleaning day and I organized the fundraising. About 35 church members of both sexes and all ages from two upwards took part.'

'Everyone who joined in the spring clean was given a badge, and anyone leaving the church without a badge was charged a Cleaning Tax.

'We publicized the cleaning day through church notices. Our only costs were church cleaning materials and a badge for each participant.'

Editors' note Although only a small amount of money was raised, this event requires little time and expenditure. It also avoids the trouble of seeking sponsors! The beauty of this event is that no one can escape – either they have to clean the church or cough up. Perhaps an extra Non-Attendance Tax could be extended to those who fail to turn up on the day!

A Mile of Coins

The public were invited to place coins (touching) in rows to equal one mile on the edge of a pavement in a busy shopping area on a Saturday.

Amount raised: £70.

Mr A. Wise, St John the Evangelist, Churchdown:

'We copied A Mile of Pennies – a fundraising event that was popular many years ago. It caught the public imagination and although we didn't raise a large sum, I think this could be a money-maker if advertised more in a public area.

'You need a lot of helpers, you need to publicize the event as early as you can and it helps to hold it in the summer. We had a church charity committee of four to organize it and we recruited help on the day. One has to stop very young children picking up the coins. They seemed to think they were on to a good thing with money laid out for the taking!'

Editors' note This is a nice idea that has been around for a long time. You may consider that given all the work involved, it isn't worth organizing for a relatively small amount of money. Perhaps it would be a good event for children to organize themselves (with some help from adults).

Charity 'Poll Tax'
A letter to all electoral roll members asking for personal donations.

Amount raised: £11,000.

Rev. Fred Carroll, Cheltenham:

'First I asked the Bishop to write to all incumbents asking if they would agree to a letter being sent to all electoral roll members appealing for personal donations, and if so, to supply the name and address of their electoral roll officer. Over half the parishes in the diocese – about 110 – agreed. A batch of letters signed by the Bishop was then sent to each officer asking for donations to be sent direct to our treasurer. (We found the numbers in the diocesan directory.)

'There was no publicity. The cost of sending batches of letters to electoral roll officers was £104.29 and the cost of copying the letters was approximately £20. If we had adopted this method at the outset, with each electoral roll member being given a sum to give or raise, we would have reached our target easily.'

Editors' note As we said at the beginning of this book, direct giving can be easily the most effective way of raising money. However there are other advantages, apart from financial ones, to organizing events – mainly that you are able to bring people into the church by encouraging their support and hopefully, later on, their actual participation in organizing the event. Also, well-publicized fundraising events help to educate the public about your cause, which is often as important, or even more important than raising money.

FOR THE CHILDREN

Any event designed for children must really appeal to them; so test the idea out on some children you know. You must make it clear from the outset whether the children will need to be accompanied by an adult during the event. Safety precautions are particularly important where children are concerned. You will need to state clearly in all your advance publicity what age group of children can take part.

Fundraising ideas for children: Balloon races, Beetle drives, Bulb-growing contests, Carol singing, Car washing, Christmas card sale (cards painted by children), Fashion show, Firework party, Halloween party, Face painting, Panto-mime, Talent contest, Treasure hunt.

Wrapping It Up

Asking children to collect pennies to purchase lengths of ribbon to wrap up Carlisle Cathedral and Cartmel Priory. On the day, wrapping up the Cathedral in ribbon and holding a carnival of music, art and drama outside. The event was designed to raise awareness about the Church Urban Fund. 500 school-age children took part.

Amount raised: Cartmel – £917, Carlisle – £911.

Miggy Scott (formerly from Carlisle):

'As we wanted to increase children's awareness of problems in the inner city areas, an Education Advisor produced materials for schools and Youth Officers organized an arts and drama project. Someone co-ordinated the musicians, we had to work out the logistics of wrapping the buildings up in ribbon and there were first aid and fire precautions!

'All the money was collected in pennies by groups of children. (We hoped to collect from passers-by, but heavy rain prevented this.) The main expense was secretarial – paper and the mailing. We confined the event to a morning to avoid major hassles over food, drink and toilets.

'Two schools were invited to measure up the buildings to see how much each circuit would raise, and this attracted a lot of media attention. Schools were given stick-on labels for the "penny jars". We encouraged frequent banking of pennies and in exchange for receipts we would measure out a length of ribbon on the day (£1 = 2 metres). The 'ribbon' was a plastic waste product several inches wide which could be written on with a waterproof marker. We used nearly two kilometres on each building.

'On the actual day, because of the torrential rain, we decided to put the ribbon inside Carlisle Cathedral but at Cartmel they stayed outside, got soaked and loved it. Their ribbon got into too big a tangle to sort out but it was great fun.

'The media were very attracted by the idea because children were involved, it was unusual and for a good cause, singer Maddy Prior took part and not a lot happens in Cumbria!'

Editors' note The idea of selling lengths of material in exchange for money raised is not a new one, but the wrapping up of a cathedral is unique! Make sure you do something imaginative with the ribbon or tape, preferably something the media can take a good photograph of. An event of this kind, which has a clear aim, really appeals to children. There is also the competitive factor – no doubt different schools and classes were trying to outdo one another's lengths of ribbon!

Sponsored Helter-Skelter

A sponsored slide down the helter-skelter at the great Hull Fair. About 40 people took part on Miss Francis Ayers's Gigantic Super Slide!

Amount raised: £640.

Rev. Allen Bagshawe, St Matthew and St Barnabas, Hull:
'The Sponsored Helter-Skelter happened very quickly. Suddenly I was on the slide and going down fast! I went to see the showmen and women at the annual Hull Fair on the Monday before it opened. By the Monday night sponsorship forms had been produced and were being distributed to some of our young people in the choir, the Beavers, Cubs and Scouts.

'We arranged it for a Sunday afternoon when local bylaws prevent the Fair from operating. Targets of 20 slides per person were set – each slide meant 52 steps up the helter-skelter!

'We got some very substantial personal sponsorships from showmen and local businesspeople. The costs were kept to a minimum because I designed the posters and sponsorship forms myself. As Chaplain to the Fair I was able to gain access to the helter-skelter at no cost for the Sunday afternoon. We all persuaded our children to join in.

'As soon as the event was fixed I sent a press release to all local media. It really caught their imagination!

'I hadn't expected to raise more than a contribution towards our parish target. We not only cleared our target but gave £150 towards that of our neighbouring parish! My only injury was a stiff right shoulder, presumably from carrying my coconut mat up all those steps! In total we climbed over 40,000 steps and made more than 800 skelters. I think the event was a world first, the afternoon was one of sheer joy.'

Editors' note Although there may not be a fairground near you, many children's play areas have small helter-skelters which would do just as well. You would need to contact the local authority to try to gain permission.

Flight of Fantasy

The chartering of a jet airliner for two flights 'to the North Pole' to meet Father Christmas.

Amount raised: £1,600.

Mr Wikeley, St Mary's, Liverpool:

'We had 101 people on each flight – mainly children – just before Christmas. Through a friendly travel agent, we managed to acquire an ABTA (Association of British Travel Agents) licence to enable us to charter the airliner. Our costs were high – £5,000 for two one-hour flights and approximately £300 for air traffic control. But we got £600 from local industry to pay for toys for the children, navigation rights and air traffic control. Each passenger paid £35.

'We sent out lots of posters and leaflets to schools in advance and we contacted the local press and radio. I feel we could have had more publicity for such an unusual idea and if I were to organize this again, I would definitely get someone in to help.

'The Bishop of Warrington was Father Christmas. We took several sick children with us as a treat, including one tetraplegic four-year-old who came with his nurse and doctor. This was paid for by his church after his doctor recommended that he should go.

'The event really was great fun. Even the pilots and cabin crew enjoyed it. But it was hard work!'

Editors' note You may live in an area where £35 for a seat on the aircraft would be out of the question for most children. It may be possible to organize a Christmas bus or train – not destined for the North Pole of course, but perhaps a day out for the children, including a surprise visit by Father Christmas. All events at this time of year can be subject to extremely cold weather.

DAREDEVIL VENTURES

By their nature, daredevil ventures often involve an element of risk. Safety precautions must be carefully looked into. Anyone taking part in an activity involving physical strain must be clear about health implications. Sometimes, as in the Viking Walk, the participants are doing something fairly normal but in fancy dress. Extroverts are attracted to events of this kind – they are easy to organize, can be free of risk and they attract a great deal of publicity.

Perhaps even more in the case of daredevil feats as in other events, you need to consider whether what you are doing will offend anyone. In the case of the jailbreaks (below), some local people were offended. How would you feel if you knew someone or had a relative in prison, if you read in the local paper that the Rotary Club had a hilarious time breaking out? You may not be concerned about your own image, but spare a few thoughts for the image of the church or organization you belong to. It is better to discuss with them what they think about the daredevil event you are planning.

Warwick Castle Breakout
Teams of two to six people were challenged to get as far as they could after being 'released' from Warwick Castle Dungeon, between 9 a.m. and 8 p.m. on a specific day, using their own resources and £10 per person.

Amount raised: £1,300.

Angus Cooper, Shottery Village:
'The purpose of the "Escape" was a joint one – to raise

95

money, but it was also a consciousness-raising event. We raised less money than we originally hoped, partly because of the low take-up and on the day it poured with archetypal Midlands rain from 7 a.m. till late at night!

'We got the agreement of Warwick Castle to use the site and we were able to put a lot of the team members down in the dungeon (a pretty noisome place) to be released by Eddie Grundy of *The Archers*. We asked everyone to wear prison garb and they nobly trudged away in the rain, wearing pyjamas with arrow heads!

'Before the event we phoned and sent out information to lots of local firms, the local police and the army. If I were to repeat the exercise, rather than contacting so many, I would target about 20 firms and really go for them. Next time, I would organize it in the summer!

'We had two hot air balloons competing – one from a private company and the other in which the Bishop of Warwick and an actress ascended. We had special trophies made and printed and I gave each competing group a watercolour painting I had done. The categories were: furthest distance, furthest and back, furthest by water, furthest vertically, most unusual and most pubs.

'In spite of the hot air balloon, the winner of the "furthest vertically" was a group who managed to climb a Welsh mountain and get back in time. A group pushed a piano into Stratford and back. We had canoeists on the Avon and a team who got to Ireland and back, while the Rolls Royce team made it to Paris.'

Bedford Jailbreak

To break out of Bedford Prison and get as far away as possible in 24 hours. Escapees were allowed no money or food and they were asked to plan their route in detail beforehand. 24 people took part.

Amount raised: £12,000.

Angela Hector, St Peter de Merton:

'Although the "prisoners" escaped from the porch of the prison, some church members felt it was a bit insensitive.

'Obviously, you need the co-operation of the prison governor in question and you should pick a day which is suitable and convenient for the prison. The local paper included a run-up to the event: "Jailbreak Plan Rumbled"; "Plans To Break Out Of Jail Not Thwarted" and so on. It was an unusual event, and it needed lots of energy, enterprise and planning during the winter months. Also, it was very exciting!

'Two police officers "escaped" to the United States. Several people got over to the continent. You need to check the credentials of participants carefully. Dressing up as clergy, even in "prison uniform" (pyjamas with arrows), can be dangerous. One couple dressed as clergy escaped with a collecting tin and haven't been seen since!'

Viking Walk

A sponsored walk by two men in full Viking costume from St James's Church, Blackburn, to the Isle of Man (including continuous walking on the deck of the ferry).

Amount raised: £1,400.

D. Hartley, St James's, Blackburn:

'This was a good fun event which attracted a lot of support and publicity, both on the Isle of Man and on this side of the water.

'We chose a Bank Holiday so that there would be a lot of traffic and passengers on the ferry. Two of us actually took part, but with help from our families. We set off at 1 a.m. and arrived at our destination at 11 p.m. the following day. The walk was 42 miles to Heysham, but 66 miles if you include walking continuously round the ferry deck!

'The local newspapers and radio were very interested by the unusual nature of the event. We were mistaken for a strippergram in Preston and we nearly frightened to death a number of drunks in the early hours of the morning.'

Editors' note This event was ideal for attracting media coverage – newspaper photographers really go for people in fancy dress, particularly something as spectacular as a Viking. So instead of doing your sponsored walk, climb, run, bike ride or jog just as you are, why not dress up?

We nearly frightened to death a number of drunks . . .

Sponsored Ride

A 16-mile, cross-country ride with two lines of optional jumps. Each rider had to produce a minimum of £5 sponsorship. 100 took part and 250 attended.

Amount raised: £1,500.

Prebendary A. Budgett, Batcombe:

'We held the sponsored ride on a Sunday in spring, when the ground would be in the best condition and we could use the maximum number of horses and ponies. There were no legal requirements, but we had to clear everything in great detail with local farmers and landowners. Most of the money was raised through sponsorship, although some of it came from the sale of refreshments. Our costs were about £200, which was spent on printing, prizes and rosettes. All the labour was voluntary.

'We had riders from a wide area across Somerset and Avon and lots of local spectators. The ride was chosen to give people the opportunity to see some very attractive countryside which was either new to them or normally inaccessible.

'The Team Rector, who had done little riding in the recent past, completed the course on a borrowed horse, but was seen moving rather stiffly around the parishes for the next few days. This was an excellent event, and we held it for two successive years with almost equal success.'

Editors' note This is a lovely event for anyone who lives in the country, or who is involved in riding. Apart from all the riding enthusiasts, you will also attract many spectators to an event of this kind. Perhaps you should consider arranging for something for the people who would like to come but who are not riders. Could you open up the stables for the children or organize pony rides? Could you arrange for a few stalls selling bric-à-brac and refreshments?

Bishop's Tower Climb

A sponsored climb of 50 church towers (plus one university tower) by the Bishop of Leicester, Rt Rev. Thomas Butler.

Amount raised: £5,500.

Bishop of Leicester:

'I climbed 50 church towers in the diocese over a period of a few days and got sponsorship for each climb. No one else took part and I organized it all myself, with secretarial help. People usually turned up to watch on the day.

'We distributed leaflets and sponsorship forms very wisely and we had generous coverage from the local media. I think they were attracted by the sight of a bishop exerting himself physically.

'On the first day of this occasionally hazardous exercise – which passed off completely safely – a fellow-bishop, standing on a chair in his kitchen, fell and badly broke his arm. This may point to a God who works in surprising ways.'

Editors' note If you can persuade your bishop, vicar, headteacher or local celebrity to do something personally, you are sure to get media coverage. Some bishops or 'celebrities' may not be able to undertake anything as strenuous as the tower climb. The 'celebrity' may come up with an idea him- or herself, but why not have a brainstorm to see if you can come up with an idea that is bound to appeal to them? Take into account their interests and hobbies and try not to dream up anything that is too demanding of their time. Get someone who knows them very well to ask them to do it.

MUSICAL EVENTS

You need not be a professional musician to take part in a musical event. The Vardy family who busked round English cathedrals attracted widespread publicity everywhere they went. Musical events are particularly likely to be covered by local radio stations, so remember to send them a press release in advance.

Busking Tour of English Cathedrals
A family (including five children aged seven to fourteen) busked in local markets and towns and then round 23 cathedrals, travelling in two Morris Minors.

Amount raised: £1,800.

Dr Vardy, Sheepwash:

'We decided to use our annual holiday to busk round the cathedrals. We are an ordinary north Devon family and not particularly talented. We played flute, trumpet, recorder and concertina. Getting families to do something together can attract a lot of publicity and good will. The media respond very well and the message can be put over widely – which we considered more important than the amount of money we raised.

'We sent a letter to the deans of cathedrals informing them of our plans. As we decided to be outside each cathedral between 10 a.m. and 12 noon on specific dates, we were able to notify the media in advance. We were provided with Church Urban Fund T-shirts to wear on the day.

'We tried to coincide our visits to small towns with market days as most people are around then. We didn't have any advance publicity in terms of attracting an audience but we had an enormous amount of coverage on television, on local radio and in the press. We wrote to each local council in advance to get permission to busk and we informed the local police of our intentions. We didn't have any costs as we were camping.

'The experience proved to be a real eye-opener. There was an Irish roadsweeper outside Oxford Cathedral who took a shine to our seven-year-old playing an Irish tune, and gave her a pound. And there was a smartly dressed lady in Salisbury who listened to us, put two pence in our box, got another one out of her purse then put it back saying, "No, I think that's enough"! Generally we found that the better dressed people were, the less they gave. And we had to stand for hours in the rain at Canterbury Cathedral being ignored by everyone until the vergers let us shelter "for ten minutes, as the canons are out of the way"!'

Editors' note Initially the Vardys were disappointed with the amount of money they raised. They depended entirely on passers-by and if the weather was bad their cap was empty. They have an enormous file of all the local coverage the family gained during their holiday and in terms of publicity alone, this was an extremely successful fundraising event.

Twelve-Hour Music Marathon

Groups and individuals made music and sang over a period of twelve hours without a break, ending with a gig by a pop group and dancing. Around 250 people took part and 1,500 attended.

Amount raised: £1,700.

John Shepherd, Mitcham Parish Church of St Peter and St Paul:

'A small committee comprising three people was set up to organize this. Jobs included writing to groups to encourage them to contribute, organizing the very many helpers, arranging the programme and publicity.

'We delivered a leaflet to every home in the parish, put up posters and contacted the local press. We were open to any type of music – solo, small groups, ensembles or choirs, classical, pop, jazz, folk. We sent a letter to children and adults asking them to take part. At the bottom of the letter was a tear-off slip which we asked them to fill in with the details and return by a certain date.

'The sale of refreshments brought in a lot of money. Our only costs were publicity and refreshments, which we took from the total raised. A lot of food was given free. Programmes were sold for 50 pence. Admission fee was £1. Top of the bill was the curate and his band Monsters of the Deep!

'This was the best money-raising event I have ever known because it brought together so many sections of the local community and it was immense fun. Standards ranged from comic to near-professional. A very gifted rock-and-roll singer took part, as did a children's playgroup. At the very end we all formed a giant conga and danced round the building!'

Editors' note The fact that the curate was a member of the band Monsters of the Deep no doubt attracted a lot of people as well as the local press. Another very appealing aspect of this event is the fact that everyone was warmly welcomed to take part – the old, the young, the experienced and the inexperienced alike. This is second to none in bringing together the whole of the local community in a wonderful fun event.

5

Fundraising and the Local Church

The first recorded example of the Church's fundraising efforts comes in the New Testament. 'I am on my way to Jerusalem', writes Paul, 'on an errand to God's people there. For Macedonia and Achaia have resolved to raise a common fund for the benefit of the poor among God's people at Jerusalem . . . For if the Jewish Christians shared their spiritual treasures with the Gentiles, the Gentiles have a clear duty to contribute to their material needs' (Romans 15 NEB).

There are many people who have already made their regular church commitment in a stewardship scheme but who would like to do even more to raise more money for other worthwhile causes. And there are others who may not be churchgoers, but who nevertheless want to help.

MORE THAN MONEY

Many good things can come out of well-organized fund-raising activity:

- People have a chance to do something practical to help others and improve the world.
- Events can focus attention on a special cause. People are far more aware of the work of Christian Aid than they are of charitable trusts that do not need to raise money.
- Events are occasions when people can work together.

- They draw out talents from people in an area which might otherwise remain unknown (even to themselves!).
- People can take responsibility in a small way. Someone may be quite happy to take charge of a cake stall or raffle but would find it hard to run the Sunday School or chair the Church Council.
- It can give an added sense of purpose to social events.
- A fundraising event or activity can be a means of drawing those on the 'fringes' of church life. Friendships and greater involvement can be the first steps towards closer identification with becoming a more committed member of the worshipping community.
- It can give a positive image of a local church concerned, helping and taking cheerful action.
- It can help the church reach out to the wider community through supporting the local school, woman's refuge or playgroup.

SENSITIVITY

Churches may need to take some extra issues into consideration when they are planning an event. There is the obvious danger that coffee mornings and events become too dominant and take attention away from committed giving.

Another danger is equally obvious. Fundraising events should be ones in which everyone can join and which do not make people feel left out. What about those who cannot afford the high entrance fee of a high-profile fundraising event? St Agnes's celebrity organ recital and dinner raised hundreds of pounds for the organ fund and was hailed by the vicar as a great fundraising success, attracting an audience from all over the city. But the churchwarden's wife, who had spent the whole afternoon the day before cleaning the church in readiness and could not afford a ticket for an event in her own church, had a very different view.

Christians disagree about raffles, prize draws, bingo and the availability of alcohol. In some churches people are happy with them, in others not. Even where churches have an agreed policy, they may cause problems where a group of churches are fundraising together. The temptation in working together for a 'good cause' is to forget how others feel.

BUILDING THE CHURCH

The wide benefits and 'spin-offs' of fundraising activity can make a special and significant contribution in the development of church life, particularly to a congregation committed to reaching out and serving the local community.

DEVELOPING SELF-CONFIDENCE

The self-confidence of individual members of the congregation can be substantially increased by setting achievable goals with results which can be seen ... and enjoyed. Imagine yourself a newcomer to church – just beginning to find your feet both in the faith and with other members of the congregation. Which seems less threatening: an invitation to read the lesson or being asked to find some sponsors for the minister's parachute jump?

Helping to organize an event can be a very safe way for people to discover their own talents and get to know those around them. Working together at something and seeing it succeed can be enormously rewarding – particularly in a church culture which too often seems to emphasize human failure and falling short.

A congregation that is more confident in itself, and at the same time sensitive to the needs of others, is more able to extend this confidence in outreach to the wider community.

STRETCHING THE MIND

Too often churches appear dull and unimaginative to the outsider, and sometimes they are. The more imagination is encouraged in the activities of church members, the more excitement and enthusiasm is going to spill over into the rest of the church's life. An imaginative membership will begin to make itself obvious in, for instance, the worship, the teaching methods of your Sunday-School teachers, the general look of the church.

Even a quick glance at the ideas and suggestions sent in by contributors to this book show that whatever else the Church lacks, it isn't imagination or talent!

What if we don't want enthusiasm and excitement?

Whatever else the Church lacks, it isn't imagination!

Imagination doesn't necessarily mean zany, madcap stunts. Imagination takes us beyond the here and now. This can involve looking backwards to a historical event (pilgrimage routes); it can be thinking geographically (cycle rides across the country); looking outwards to other cultures (African lunches). Above all it is taking people one step further and taking them beyond their everyday experience.

The recycled church of St Mark's, Biggin Hill was built entirely from the stones of a redundant bombed church which was moved stone by stone from Camberwell to be rebuilt on the new site. Thirty years later a sponsored walk was held along the same route taken by the stones. Historically imaginative, this excellent idea took the people back into their own church's past and into the heart of inner-city Camberwell. In one fell swoop, the people of St Mark's learned more, not only about the struggles of their past, but about the particular pressures facing people living in Camberwell today.

REACHING THE COMMUNITY

One of the consequences of many fundraising events is an increase in contact with the very people the church may be aiming to reach. People who live in the area but have never stepped inside the church building; people who know someone who goes to church, but have never understood why.

There are several stages to a church's development of links with the local community through fundraising:

- People notice what you are doing and increasingly respect the work of the church, because the church is seen to care for others.
- The church is doing something which is a success.
- People begin to feel responsible for the success (or otherwise) of the fundraising campaign when they become involved in the planning.
- People initiate ideas, perhaps for the first time. Try to take them up and use them wherever possible.
- People begin to trust the church; it is no longer remote and daunting. It becomes their church.

EQUIPPING THE SAINTS

Organizing fundraising activities and events is most valuable when it engages a variety of people in different ways:

- People who are most actively involved in the organization, whose talents may be being used for the first time. Nobody ever knew Moira was good at woodwork, but here she is making the set for the pantomime. Everybody has a gift; it's a matter of finding out what it is and unlocking the door ...

- People working together for a common goal have a sense of having achieved something. So important, too, that the group remains fluid. We may all enjoy working with the same group of people year after year, but what about all those other people, whose talents we aren't using, who may feel excluded?

- Potential leaders. There are some people who always seem to emerge as leaders, who motivate people, who are good at discovering hidden talents and don't always end up sighing 'Well, I suppose I'll have to do it myself'; people who are good at recognizing and giving way to leadership qualities in others, who are good at recognizing when people are overstretched.

- The people involved on the edges are just as important. They are the people who may not have time to take part fully but want to feel they've done their bit. They are potential supporters, the ones who may do an hour on a stall between midday and one o'clock.

- The children. Are they made to feel welcome? Are they given jobs to do? It's amazing what a toddler can do to help when give a small job. Are children's ideas taken up? Are you helping them to organize their own events?

- Other groups working in the same area. This could be a marvellous opportunity to involve the Brownies, the local Tenants Association or the church round the corner.

- The people who come to the event or sponsor a participant. This may be the first time in years they've had anything to do with the church. An event organized for a special cause may help people to learn what you are about. Here's a church which looks outwards – the people in it think I'm worth talking to.

- The wider public. Nobody should feel excluded. Try

to organize different types of events to appeal to different types of people. So, you had a disco last time; what about having a sponsored knit next time? How about a sponsored funday, where everybody is being sponsored for whatever they do best – bagpipe playing, cycling round the park, silence ... Do you make sure that people with disabilities can take part? Is your committee representative of the people who live in the area?

CELEBRATING CREATION

The overwhelming experience of the contributors to this book is that fundraising can be rewarding, worthwhile and fun! There is something particularly satisfying about that moment when everyone starts to arrive, or you cross the finishing line, and you realize that all the preparations have paid off. The committee meetings, the pieces of paper and the endless phone calls give way to a lively happening with people openly enjoying themselves.

Mitres and Minors

6

Avoiding Trouble

Fundraising is fun. Whether your event involves only one or two people or the whole community, you want everyone to really enjoy themselves as well as raising money for your cause. With a little thought beforehand, you can avoid the headaches that can arise as a result of bad planning.

KEEP IT LEGAL

Many events do not stick to the strict letter of the law in every detail. Most of the time, as long as the event poses no danger, doesn't cause a nuisance and there are no complaints, the authorities will not make a fuss. Always bear in mind that you must not put the public at risk in any way and that no basic rights should be infringed.

WHICH CHARITY?

Whether you are raising money for famine relief, a lunch club, activity holidays for young people or the local Scouts, it is usually advisable to work through an existing charity. They will be able to provide you with leaflets both about the charity itself and about the issues it is concerned with. If the charity is a membership organization, it is always a good idea to distribute leaflets so that people can join it if they wish to make a more long-term commitment. If you are collecting money on behalf of a charity, they will be able to equip you with the necessary items such as collecting tins, flags or badges.

If you are raising money for a specific project, you may

want to consider registering for charitable status with the Charity Commission. Once you have registered, you are entitled to the rate and tax advantages of a charity. If you do want to start up a new charity, send for leaflet No CC21, from the Charity Commission, St Alban's House, 57–60 Haymarket, London SW1Y 4QX. This leaflet contains guidelines on how to do so.

The Charities Act 1992 makes provision for the prevention of unauthorized fundraising. No matter how harmless the event, make sure you ask permission from your chosen charity before you embark on a fundraising event on their behalf. They can allow you to use their name and they may wish to make some suggestions about the nature of the event.

NO OFFENCE MEANT

You may cause offence by organizing certain events, even if this is the last thing you intended to do. It is worth sparing a little time to think about any aspect of your event which could cause offence to anyone, bearing in mind the area in which you live and who will be taking part. One of the contributors to this book describes how some local people felt that the jailbreak they had organized was a little insensitive to the feelings of actual prisoners nearby. Events to be handled with care include: any event in a multi-ethnic area; gambling events and lotteries; lavish feasts.

You would clearly be courting bad publicity if you decided to hold a pie-eating contest in aid of starving people. This may sound absurd, but it is surprisingly easy to overlook such hostages to fortune. What if the local hunt were to organize an event in support of an animal welfare charity opposed to hunting?

COLLECTIONS

You cannot hold a collection wherever you like, and if you hold one on private property you must have permission from the owner. There are many places where people can be easily approached and asked to give – outside churches or cinemas, in pubs, in railways or in busy shopping centres. If you are holding an open-air meeting you don't need a permit for the collection but you do need to apply for permission to hold the event from your local authority.

The Local Government Act 1972 empowers local authorities to regulate collections on public property and there may be slight variations around the country as to how they do this. You need to apply in writing to the administration department of the Council covering the area you wish to collect in, at least a month ahead of the event.

LOCAL BRANCHES

If you are collecting money for a branch of a charity rather than a national organization, you will need to find out if the local branches are legally separate from the national organization. If so, you will need to apply for a permit from the relevant local authority. Where the branches are legally independent, the national charity can authorize the branches to collect on its behalf. In this case, the money would all be paid to the national charity, but the charity could then (depending on the nature of the appeal) make grants to the local branches.

STREET COLLECTIONS

Only one organization can hold a collection on any one day and the collection must take place during the times stated on the permit. Collections can be limited to one street or cover a whole area. Anyone who has a collecting box has to stay stationary and must not coerce passers-by in any way. The boxes have to be sealed (as we said before, you will normally be able to obtain these from the charity of your choice). All collectors must be 16 or over. You may be required to submit to the Council a list of the collectors and how much was raised.

HOUSE TO HOUSE

If you are collecting money house-to-house or carol-singing, you also need a permit, which you can get from the local authority. A house-to-house collection is also governed by a set of regulations.

COLLECTING BOXES

If the collecting box is placed on private property, no permit is required, although you do need the permission of the owner. This allows you to put collecting boxes in shopping centres or railway stations, *or* you could get smaller boxes placed on shopping counters, on the bar in a pub or in your local building society.

Remember: if you are collecting in public, your collectors will be your ambassadors. Make sure they all know why they are asking for money and what the money raised is for. If you are collecting house-to-house, collectors need to be equipped with information about your organization and they need to be brief, interesting and persuasive.

INSURANCE

Public liability

No matter how small the event you are organizing, you need to have Public Liability Insurance cover. This applies to the most popular summer events like car-boot sales and school fêtes. 'But we're only organizing a coffee morning in my garden. There will only be about 20 people there.' You are still taking a risk. What if a kettle of scalding water topples and someone is badly burnt?

Public Liability Insurance will cover you against any claim that you were negligent in organizing some aspect of the event. You are not required by law to take out insurance cover, but for a relatively small sum (as little as £20) you could save yourself a lot of trouble.

Rainfall

If you are holding an event outside, you can insure against rainfall. This will cover your fixed costs, such as hiring charges, labour costs or publicity, if your event is cancelled due to rain, hail or snow.

All risks, money and personal assault

This will cover you against damage or theft to property, the theft of money or an attack on helpers at the event.

Some companies specialize in more unusual events such as art exhibitions, horse shows, street processions, festivals and concerts. Unless you are absolutely certain which is the best company to provide what you need, it is probably best to use a broker.

GETTING A LICENCE

If you intend to sell alcohol you will need to apply for a Liquor Licence and you will need an Entertainments Licence for anything where music or dancing is the main event. Raffles and gambling must comply with the Lotteries Act. If you are in any doubt about what licence you need, seek advice. All that is usually needed is a phone call to the appropriate licensing authority.

SELLING ALCOHOL

If you want to sell alcohol you will need to apply to the local Magistrates' Court who take advice from the police. If you are using a building that already has a licence you should have no problems, provided the licensee is present during the event. In an unlicensed building or at an outside event, you are unlikely to be granted a licence. You will need to approach a person who has a full 'on-licence' and ask him/her to apply for an extension for the duration of the event.

ENTERTAINMENTS

The law states that where two or more people are performing or where dancing is taking place, a Public Entertainments Licence is required. The main areas of concern are fire escapes, exits and procedures for getting people out of the building, noise pollution and the safety of electrical fittings.

In order to get a Public Entertainments Licence you need to apply to the Licensing Section of your local authority. You will have to ensure that you have adequate fire exits before you apply. There will be a charge of usually between £100 and £200. The local authority will inform the Chief Fire Officer, the Police and the Environmental Health Department. As there is a wait, you would be well advised

Sporting Dinner

You will need an extension to the licence (see p.79)

to consult your local authority at least three months in advance if you can. If your application is successful you can proceed according to plan. You may be given conditions that will need to be met on the day of the event.

CHURCH HALLS

If you are going to hold your event in a church hall, pub or community centre, you may find that the building already has a Public Entertainments Licence and all you have to do is comply with it.

If the building you have chosen does not already have a licence, you will have to apply for a temporary Public Entertainments Licence. You will need to apply several months in advance in case you are unsuccessful the first time. Always avoid buildings near hospitals or sheltered accommodation.

OUTSIDE EVENTS

If the event consists mainly of performances you will definitely need a Public Entertainments Licence. In built-up areas you may have complaints before the event and the Environmental Protection Officers may get involved. If you are expecting several hundred people to turn up and there is entertainment of some kind – even if it is not the main event – you will need to seek advice.

SUNDAY TRADING LAWS

Sunday trading laws can be very problematic for fêtes, fairs and car-boot sales, depending on where you live. Every local authority makes its own interpretation of the Shops Act 1950, which places restrictions on Sunday trading. Some councils prosecute while others ignore all sales on Sundays. Unless you are sure that you are not going to run into any trouble, it may be wise to organize a sale on another day.

HEALTH AND SAFETY

If you are planning to hold a large event at which a large number of people will be helping, paid or unpaid, it is worth getting a hold of a government publication called *Essentials of Health and Safety at Work*. This gives good, easy to follow guidelines on how to avoid hazards and what to do in emergencies. The Health and Safety at Work Act covers not only those in paid formal employment, but anybody and everybody working with the public, whether paid or unpaid.

NO ACCIDENTS PLEASE!

You have a responsibility to all the people who take part in your fundraising event to keep them safe. All too easily, a fun day can be spoiled by an accident: someone scalds their hand on the tea urn, a child falls off the helter-skelter, an elderly person trips over a wire and falls downstairs. Here is a list which might help to avoid accidents during the event:

- Have all electrical appliances checked.
- Make sure there are no piles of rubbish which could be set alight.
- Restrict access to cookers, boiling water or soup and tea urns.
- Check for cables across walkways, loose ropes or tent pegs.
- Make sure pedestrians do not use routes for vehicles.
- Ask for St John Ambulance or the Red Cross to assist at large events.
- Ask lifeguards to be present at any event by the sea.
- Make sure that two people transport money to banks.
- Check all routes for possible hazards before the event.
- Check for steep drops and unfenced paths.

BOUNCY CASTLES

There are no laws governing bouncy castles but they are so popular at outside events, it is worth saying a few words about them – in warning! Many children are injured in bouncy castles each year. The castles have been known to take off, so make sure they are firmly tied down with ropes. Limit the time that each group of children can bounce and only allow a small group to bounce at any one time. Try to organize groups of children of around the same size and age. Make sure an adult is inside the castle at all times to help in the event of an accident. Safety guidelines are available from the Health and Safety Executive, HSE Guidance Note PM76 from HMSO stockists.

DON'T OVERDO IT

Some of the fundraising ideas in this book are very strenuous and physically challenging. This doesn't meant that everyone who takes part in a fundraising event has to be in tip-top condition. You don't have to be able-bodied and you don't have to have spent the last year in a gym to raise money for your favourite charity. But you do need to know just how fit you are and what kind of challenge you are taking on.

Bill Purchase ran the whole length of Britain at the age of 55, but he spent months in training beforehand. A sick child took part in the Flights of Fantasy but was accompanied by a nurse. Pam Richardson, a cancer survivor, undertook a marathon walk, but she knew when she set off she was fit and well and able to do so.

Always make sure that in all your promotional literature you tell people how far they are expected to walk, run or cycle. Tell them if the event is suitable for children or elderly people or whether you have arranged for disabled access. Never try to persuade or cajole anyone into taking part in an event they feel unsure about. Nowadays, daredevil events like bungee-jumping are commonplace. Not everyone is fit enough or brave enough to participate. Don't take risks! It simply isn't worth it!

Useful Addresses

(In phone numbers, the code in brackets (e.g. 071–) is for use until 16 April 1995, when it is replaced by the code preceding the brackets: e.g. 0171–)

Charitable organizations
Charities Advisory Trust, Radius Works, Back Lane, London NW3 1HL (Christmas card service)   Tel: 0171(071)–435 6523

Charities Aid Foundation, 48 Pembury Road, Tonbridge, Kent TN9 2JE   Tel: 01732(0732)–771333

Charity Christmas Card Council, 221 St John Street, London EC1V 4LY   Tel: 0171(071)–336 7476

Charity Commission, St Alban's House, 57–60 Haymarket, London SW1Y 4QX   Tel: 0171(071)–210 3000

Christian Aid, Interchurch House, 35 Lower Marsh, London SE1 7RG   Tel: 0171(071)–620 4000

National Council for Voluntary Organisations, Regents Wharf, All Saints Street, London N1 9RL Tel: 0171(071)–713 6161

Goods and services
The Amazing Bunting Company, PO Box 274, Northampton NN3 9AD   Tel: 01604(0604)–786655

Angal Ltd (collecting boxes, flags), 68 First Avenue, London SW14 8SR   Tel: 0181(081)–788 5464

Barnums Carnival Novelties, 67 Hammersmith Road, London W14 8UZ   Tel: 0171(071)–602 1211

Crafts Council, 44a Pentonville Road, Islington, London N1 9BY   Tel: 0171(071)–278 7700

Kimbolton Fireworks, 7 High Street, Kimbolton, Hunts PE18 0HB   Tel: 01480(0480)–860988

The Kite and Balloon Company, 160 Eardley Road, London SW16 5TG   Tel: 0181(081)–679 8844

Restroom Rentals (loos) Tel 01132(0532)–639081 for your nearest office

SGB Readyfence   Tel: 0181(081)–628 3400 for your nearest office

Shell Shock Fireworks Company, South Manor Farm, Bramfield, Halesworth, Suffolk IP19 9AQ Tel: 0198(098)–684407

Standard Fireworks, Standard Drive, Crosland Hill, Huddersfield HD4 7AD   Tel: 01484(0484)–640640

Ticket shop (official tickets), 13 Cremyll Road, Reading, Berkshire RG1 8NQ   Tel: 01734(0734)–599234

Wall's Carnival Stores, 155 Caversham Road, Reading, Berks RG1 8BB   Tel: 01734(0734)–586727

Webb Ivory Ltd, Queensbridge Works, Queen Street, Burton on Trent DE14 3LP   Tel: 01283(0283)–66311

Media

BBC Appeal Office, Broadcasting House, Portland Place, London W1A 1AA   Tel: 0171(071)–765 4562

BBC Radio, Broadcasting House, Portland Place, London W1A 1AA   Tel: 0171(071)–580 4468

BBC TV, Television Centre, Wood Lane, London W12 7RJ Tel: 0181(081)–743 8000

The Catholic Communications Centre, 136 Victoria Street, London SW1E 5LD   Tel: 0171(071)–233 8196

Catholic Herald, Herald House, Lamb's Passage, Bunhill Row, London EC1Y 8TQ   Tel: 0171(071)–588 3101

The Church of England Newspaper, 10 Little College Street, London SW1P 3SH   Tel: 0171(071)–976 7760

Church House Communications Unit, Church House, Great Smith Street, London SW1P 3NZ Tel: 0171(071)–222 9011

Church Times, 33 Upper Street, London N1 0PN   Tel: 0171(071)–359 4570

Methodist Recorder, 122 Golden Lane, London EC1Y 0TL   Tel: 0171(071)–251 8414

The Universe, 1st Floor, St James's Buildings, Oxford Street, Manchester M1 6FP   Tel: 0161(061)–236 8856

Other

AA Signs Service, Fanum House, Dogkennel Lane, Halesowen, West Midlands B63 3BT   Tel: 0800–393808

Gaming Board of Great Britain, Berkshire House, 168 High Holborn, London WC1V 7AA   Tel: 0171(071)–306 6200

The Performing Right Society, 29–33 Berners Street, London W1P 4AA   Tel: 0171(071)–580 5544

Phonographic Performance Ltd, 14 Ganton Street, London W1V 1LB   Tel: 0171(071)–437 0311 (permission to use recorded music)

RAC Motor Sports Association, Motor Sports House, Riverside Park, Colnbrook, Slough SL3 0HG Tel: 01753(0753)–681736

RAC Signs Service, RAC House, M1 Cross, Brent Terrace, London NW2 1LT   Tel: 0800–234810

Ramblers Association, 1–5 Wandsworth Road, London SW8 2LX   Tel: 0171(071)–582 6878

St John Ambulance, 1 Grosvenor Crescent, London SW1X 7EF   Tel: 0171(071)–235 5231

Mowbray Parish Handbooks

An ABC for the PCC: A Handbook for Church Council Members, *3rd edition*
  John Pitchford
Adult Way to Faith: A Practical Handbook with Resources to Photocopy
  Peter Ball
Appointed for Growth: A Handbook of Ministry Development and Appraisal
  Kevin Eastell (ed.)
Handbook for Churchwardens and Parochial Church Councillors, *1989 edition*
  Kenneth Macmorran, E. Garth Moore and T. Briden
Handbook of Parish Finance, *3rd edition*
  Phyllis Carter and Michael Perry
Handbook of Parish Worship, *revised edition*
  Michael Perry
Handbook of Pastoral Work, *revised edition*
  Michael Hocking
Handbook of Sick Visiting
  Norman Autton
Learning for Life: A Handbook of Adult Religious Education
  Yvonne Craig
Spring into Action: A Handbook of Local Fundraising
  Martin Field and Alison Whyte (eds)
Yours, Lord: A Handbook of Christian Stewardship
  Michael Wright

In preparation
Community Work: A Handbook for Volunteer Groups and Local Churches
  Malcolm Grundy